Smith H. Platt

The Power of Grace over Acquired Habits, Special Inborn Perversities and the Natural Appetites

Smith H. Platt

The Power of Grace over Acquired Habits, Special Inborn Perversities and the Natural Appetites

ISBN/EAN: 9783337814090

Printed in Europe, USA, Canada, Australia, Japan

Cover: Foto ©Lupo / pixelio.de

More available books at **www.hansebooks.com**

THE
POWER OF GRACE

OVER

ACQUIRED HABITS, SPECIAL INBORN PERVERSITIES, AND THE NATURAL APPETITES.

"The flesh lusteth against the spirit, and the spirit against the flesh; and these are contrary the one to the other." Gal. 5. 17. "Know ye not that your body is the temple of the Holy Ghost which is in you, which ye have of God, and ye are not your own? For ye are bought with a price; therefore glorify God in your body and in your spirit which are God's." 1 Cor. 6. 19, 20. "Let us cleanse ourselves from all filthiness of the flesh and spirit." 2 Cor. 7. 1.

BY

REV. S. H. PLATT, A.M.,

Author of "The Gift of Power;" "Christ and Adornments;" "Christian Separation from the World;" "The Philosophy of Christian Holiness;" "The Man of Like Passions," or "Elijah the Tishbite;" "The Wondrous Name;" "The Christian Law of Giving;" "To every Man his Work," &c.

BROOKLYN, N. Y. :
S. HARRISON & CO
1874.

Entered according to act of Congress, in the year 1874, by
S. H. PLATT,
in the office of the Librarian of Congress, at Washington, D. C.

Introduction.

It is the misfortune of most men to reach the years of mature judgment after an incipient training in some one or more species of Perversion, and to find themselves then manacled by evil Habits of one kind or another, to break away from which requires all the energy and persistent efforts of their manhood.

And too frequently, the struggle is felt to be hopeless from the outset, and the work of undoing is consequently begun so feebly, that it amounts to little more than an inefficient protest against a bondage that continues unbroken to the end. Hence, life is full of sails drifting, in more or less dismantled conditions, on the lee shore of ruin.

Vain the flying storm-signals! Vain the ringing fog-bells! Vain the booming distress-guns! The drift is shoreward still. There the breakers dash! And there Destruction lurks!!

Is there any help?

If the Gospel be not a mockery, its glorious challenge to misfortune, fatality and despair—"*All things are possible to him that believeth!*"—is a RINGING SHOUT OF HELP AT HAND!

Read and know.

The testimonies contained in these pages are in response to the following questions published by the Author, in various religious journals, in September, 1874:

1. Can persons of nervous temperament be so kept by the power of grace that, in times of continuous strain of duties while in a state of nervous exhaustion, they shall be free from all sense of irritability?

2. Is the *felt* irritability of temper, which often results from disordered bodily conditions, consistent with a holy heart?

3. Can men be instantaneously delivered from the power of *acquired* habits, such as the use of tobacco, rum, etc., so that they shall thereafter have no craving for the indulgence?

4. May those in whom the craving for narcotics or stimulants is *inborn*, and almost as a natural appetite, expect deliverance from the desire, in answer to prayer for purifying grace?

5. Can the strongest appetite of the human organism be so subdued in a moment, by the power of the Holy Spirit, that thereafter solicitation to indulgence shall not disturb the peace of the soul?

6. When, by reason of parental misfortune or perversity, that appetite is inborn in the child, and grows with his growth, can he hope, at any period of his vigorous manhood, for such deliverance as thereafter to rest from frequent or almost constant soul-harassing conflict with desire?

THE POWER OF GRACE.

CHAPTER I.

ALL who believe in Divine Grace as a gift of God to man, admit a greater or less efficiency in it to accomplish the ends for which it was given. Much of our faith upon this subject is derived from the Holy Scriptures, which present its power under a great variety of aspects, and by means of the most expressive figures.

Personal experience confirms the testimony of the Bible, changes the faith into knowledge, and renders the knowledge exact and discriminating. That knowledge *expressed* becomes *human testimony*, which is of greater or less value according to the circumstances of the case. When given upon matters of personal knowledge; by those of sufficient intelligence adequately to comprehend the facts; of sufficient integrity to intend fairly to report them; so far free from prejudices warping judgment, and from influences controling decision, that truth to facts may be presumed to be practically attainable; and when all this is found in connection with ample opportunity to *investigate;* and moreover, in such circumstances that, according to the ordinary laws of mind, investigation is *imperative;* when, in addition to all this, there is NO *rebutting evidence* of FACTS, it is clear that *such testimony must be received without serious abatement as to matters of fact.*

To affirm the contrary would be to unsettle all legal proceedings, uproot all historical evidence, destroy the very foundations of every natural science, and henceforth render the acceptance of testimony upon any subject impossible. If, then, we have SUCH TESTIMONY to offer in this treatise, the mere fact that it is brought in contact with the intelligence of the reader, places him immediately under a double obligation, viz.: First, to *honor* God by a manly *acceptance* of this testimony. Second, to honor God by *confessing* his *conscience* to be bound by the law of that testimony. Nor can any plea of evasion avail. It is an open, square demand on the part of FACT (God's great Revelator), to be admitted within the domain of accepted things; and denial can be nothing short of treason to manliness, and rebellion against moral obligation.

But suppose the testimony to be admitted, what then?

The facts affirmed DETERMINE the MEASURE of the power of grace so far as it has been applied in these particular instances. It may be needed equally as much in other instances. How shall we know? That it is needed in overcoming inborn perversities, none can doubt. That it is *sometimes* needed in the control of acquired habits and natural appetites will be freely conceded, and by these rules let us ascertain WHEN!

WHEN HUMAN WILL AND ENERGY REQUIRE AID TO MASTER ANY HABITS OR APPETITES THAT EXHIBIT THE FOLLOWING FEATURES, viz.:

1. When they demand indulgences

that must tend toward disease, by the operation of the chemical and physiological laws brought into play.

2. When they call for indulgences that tend directly, and of natural consequence, to induce other habits of an injurious character.

3. When their indulgence transmits to posterity diseased conditions and perverted tendencies.

4. When indulgence is, of its own nature, so strengthening to selfishness, that spiritual interests are thereby sacrificed.

To affirm that habits or appetites, the indulgence of which involves either of these four classes of consequences, may be innocently permitted in any case *merely* as a self-gratification, is to deny all moral responsibility for our acts, and enthrone Desire as the Law-giver of our lives. For, if we may injure ourselves physically for no good end, and voluntarily load others with needless infirmities and sufferings, and of set purpose subordinate our spiritual natures to our fleshly lusts, then is the great Law of Love abrogated, and

Passion and Caprice are become the High Priests of our Destiny.

Few will have the hardihood to assume such a position.

If, then, the law of obligation demands of those whose habits are entailing either of the four consequences stated, an abandonment of such habits, and if the facts attested demonstrate the sovereignty of grace over similar habits in the experience of others, then does the *overmastering power of grace* (through prayer) become the sheet-anchor of hope to all such.

For the sake of others, then, if not for himself, let the reader peruse this little treatise to the end.

CHAPTER II.

THE POWER OF GRACE IN ERADICATING ACQUIRED HABITS.

EXPERIENCE proves that the power of habit is so great, that it can only be broken by the most decisive measures. We call attention to but few of the many acquired habits to which men are in subjection, considering these as representative of the whole.

SECTION 1. THE TOBACCO HABIT.

Ought it to be eradicated? In some cases, perhaps in most, it certainly should.

If there are any doubtful examples, they may be settled by an application of the rules already laid down; which we proceed to do carefully and without prejudice.

(1.) Does its indulgence tend toward

disease, by the operation of the chemical and physiological laws brought into play ?

Tobacco (*Nicotiana Tobacum*), says the Encyclopedia Americana, is "a nauseous and poisonous weed of an acrid taste and disagreeable odor, whose only properties are deleterious." The analysis of M. Posselt and Kiemann show the leaf to be composed as follows : Nicotine 0·07 ; extractive matter 2·87 ; gum 1·74 ; a green resin 0·27 ; albumen 0·26 ; gluten 1·05 ; malic acid 0·51; malate of ammonia 0·12 ; sulphate of potash 0·05 ; chloride of potassium 0·06 ; nitrate and malate of potash 0·21 ; phosphate of lime 0·17 ; malate of lime 0·72 ; silica 0·09 ; woody matter 4·97; and water 86·84=100·00. During the fermentation of the leaves there is always a formation of ammoniacal salts.

These elements yield three constituents when the tobacco is burned, either in pipes or cigars, viz. :

1. About two grains to the pound, of a volatile oil, causing, when swallowed, giddiness and nausea.

2. A volatile alkali — nicotine — from three to eight per cent., one of the most

deadly poisons known, and scarcely inferior to prussic acid.

3. An empyreumatic oil, produced during combustion, and so poisonous that a single drop on the tongue of a cat will cause death in two minutes, by operating directly upon the brain and nervous system like prussic (hydrocyanic) acid, while nicotine and the volatile oil act chiefly through the motor nerves and paralyze the heart. Hence says Dr. Waterhouse: "We know of no animal that can resist its mortal effects."

So dangerous and potent are its narcotic properties that it is seldom used for any purpose in medicine; and, when used, the greatest caution is necessary; for, even when administered by a faithful physician. *it has in many cases produced fatal results.* A single drop of nicotine has been found to kill a dog, and small birds have quickly perished at the approach of a tube containing it. One drop destroyed a half-grown cat in five minutes. Two drops on the tongue of a red squirrel destroyed it in one minute. A small puncture made in the tip of the nose with a surgeon's needle, bedewed with the oil of tobacco, caused death in six minutes. Two drops of nicotine, injected into the jugular vein of a dog, have been found to act in ten seconds, proving fatal in two minutes and a half.

Put a victim of the tobacco habit into a hot bath; let full and free perspiration arise; then drop a fly into the water—and the fly dies at the instant of contact; so, leeches are instantly poisoned by the blood of smokers. Cannibals will not eat human flesh which contains the flavor of tobacco. Even the turkey-buzzards of Mexico refused the flesh of soldiers addicted to this indulgence!

These tobacco-essences are constantly being given off by insensible perspiration, and this is so abundant as sometimes to seriously affect the health of a bed-companion.

Dr. Higginbottom, of Nottingham, gives this testimony after fifty years of extensive practice: "Tobacco in every form has no redeeming property whatever, and at the present time is a main cause of ruining young men, pauperizing working men, and rendering useless the best efforts of ministers of religion."

J. Ronald Martin, F. R. S., a great living authority in diseases incident to warm countries, states from his own observation, that the miseries, mental and bodily, produced by cigar-smoking, chiefly in young men, far exceed anything detailed in the "Confessions of an Opium-Eater."

Says Dr. Solly: "I know of no *single* vice which does so much harm."

The German physicians state that of the deaths occurring among men in that country, between eighteen and thirty-five years of age, one half die from the effects of smoking.

Dr. Trall declares that, "Many an infant has been killed outright in its cradle by the tobacco smoke with which a thoughtless father filled an unventilated room."

I was myself a witness to one such case in the city of Brooklyn, N. Y., when called to baptize a dying child, whose life was sacrificed to its father's love of smoke.

So depressing is it to the power of life, that it is declared on good authority that in the experience of prize runners (even those who at all times, except when training, are addicted to its use), one-third of a cigar, smoked the day before a race of two hundred yards, *will diminish the speed by ten yards.*

Such being its properties, it is not surprising that Nature guards against its introduction into the human system by all the distressing symptoms attending its use at first.

The experience of Dr. J. C. Jackson, as given in his " Tobacco and its Effects," may be taken as representative:

" As soon as I was able to realize the responsibility of my life in the feeblest degree, manhood was the state which was always presented to me for my consideration, and every motive that could be brought to bear upon me to its attainment was made effective. To be a *man*, not a child ; to be a *man*, not a boy ; to be a *man*, not a youth ; was represented as the chief good after which I was to seek. Of course my mind became preternaturally active and morbidly sensitive in respect to the accomplishment of this great object, and as I saw that social position had its symbols and types of recognition, and among these was the use of tobacco, either in the form of chewing or smoking, or more generally both, I determined to bridge the chasm which separated me from the manly, and to become, let what would happen to me, one of the initiated.

"It was as beautiful a Sabbath morning in June as ever the sun shone upon in our clime, when I resolved, with all the fervor and energy characterizing my nature, to make the attempt. My father had a hired man of middle age who was himself a great tobacco-chewer, never using it in any other form. He advised me to commence by chewing, gave me directions about it, telling me what I must expect, announcing to me that I should be deadly sick, but that it would not last a great while, when I got over it, I must immediately take another chew into my mouth, which would make me even sicker than before, and after this sickness passed away I should have little or no further trouble.

"Our house was a modest farm-house,

facing the public street, and shaded by beautiful locust trees. In front of the door was a large flat stone, and just before the threshold, on either side, stood two locust trees shading the doorway. When our family had all gone to church, sitting down upon that stone and looking up through the opening spaces of the trees overhead, I introduced this poison into my veins. So far as I ever had consciousness of my conditions, they are as vivid to me now as they were on that morning, and no language of which I am the owner can begin to describe the terrible suffering through which, on that blessed Sabbath day, I passed. No effort that I have ever since made to secure to myself position with my fellows, to work out for myself a manly character, which should challenge the public confidence, have been marked by a more decided self-abnegation or greater sublimity of spiritual feeling than I exhibited on that day. I had not only no thoughts of educating myself into a vicious habit, but on the other hand, I earnestly sought to possess myself of a means of becoming, though young, more respected and honored by every person whose respect and good will I was desirous to obtain. I do not believe that my heart ever went out in more earnest devotion, nor that I ever more sincerely prayed to Heaven to help me succeed in any effort that I was about to enter upon, than I did on that occasion. In five minutes my saliva had mingled with the tobacco which I had put into my mouth, and I began to be blind. In a little while after, I seemed to be thrown into illimitable space, driven on by forces of which I had no knowledge, but which were omnipotent, and for the better part of a life-time, as it *then* seemed, I drifted hither and thither, without the least self-control. I think no human being was ever more thoroughly intoxicated than I was. While I retained, in extreme measure, consciousness of what passed on the occasion, there were no relations to personal existence which at the time were not, and ever since have not, been largely chaotic. How long, in fact, I was in that condition, I do not know, but probably not a great while, when insensibility ensued, and I lay down upon the flagstone, and there remained, until, at length, under the reaction of the Vital Forces, consciousness returned, and I looked about and gradually found where I was.

"The battle was *half* fought. I immediately opened my mouth and took another chew, when blindness and deafness ensued, twitching of the muscles, and deadly sickness, with severe prostration, followed, and I again became insensible. It was ten o'clock when I first seated myself and entered upon my matriculation; it was half-past two o'clock when I came out of the last fit of insensibility. Dragging myself into the house by my hands, as a person would whose lower limbs had suddenly become paralyzed, I reached our pantry, and there found some cold coffee, which had been set aside from breakfast, and of which I drank largely, after the directions of my father's hired man, previously given. Soon I became relieved from my great nervous and muscular depression and was able to get up."

Why all these symptoms *then*, and not at a later period?

The answer is found in this :

"The grand characteristic of all narcotic substances, is their *anti-vital* or life-destroying property. When they are not so highly concentrated or energetic as to destroy life instantly, they produce the most powerful and often the most violent and distressing vital reaction, which also causes a corresponding degree of exhaustion, depression and prostration ; and they often destroy life purely by vital exhaustion in this violent and continued vital reaction. But when the discriminating sensibilities of the system have been depraved by the habitual use of these substances, and its power of giving a sympathetic alarm greatly impaired, these same substances, even the most deadly in nature, if the quantity be only commensurate with the degree of physiological depravity, may be habitually introduced and even received into the general circulation, and diffused over the whole system, and slowly but surely destroy the constitution, and always greatly increase the liability to disease, and almost certainly create it, and invariably aggravate it, without any of those symptoms which are ordinarily considered as the evidences of the action of poison on a living body; but on the contrary, their stimulation is attended with that pleasurable feeling and agreeable mental consciousness which lead the mind to the strongest confidence in their salutary nature and effects."— *Graham's Science of Human Life.*

Hence it follows, that the strength of the appetite may be regarded as a correct indication of the injury which it has already wrought in the system, since that appetite is solely the effect of the "physiological depravity" that has been induced in creating it. This is a most important fact, which certainly ought to disturb the "pleasurable feeling and agreeable mental consciousness which lead the mind to the strongest confidence in their salutary nature and effects."

If its killing power does not fix upon a single organ, it gradually diminishes the healthy forces, ending in general disease and premature age; or, allowing its devotee to look firm and robust, it finally severs the thread of life with a sudden, unexpected stroke, which is thus explained by Dr. Twitchell:

"The nerves of involuntary motion—those whose function it is to carry on the action of the lungs, heart and stomach—are placed beyond the power of the will, acting without our consciousness, in sleep as well as when awake; and it is upon these the habitual use of tobacco produces its most pernicious effects, by paralyzing their action.

"It first manifests itself in the respiration, which is imperfectly performed; the blood is not fully purified, and a sense of anxiety or incipient suffocation is felt; to relieve which a voluntary effort is made to expand the chest to take in more air; and, every now and then, a deep inspiration or sigh is the result, giving momentary relief.

"But, during sleep, especially when first going to sleep, the will not being so easily excited to action, the sense of suffocation is longer endured, till, at length becoming painful, a degree of consciousness is awakened; the individual begins to feel his condition, and rouses, perhaps suddenly starts, and sits up in the bed in alarm, his heart palpitating violently; and, having obtained relief, soon goes to sleep, to pass through the same scenes again.

"But, as the habit continues, the whole nervous system becomes affected; the muscles become tremulous, the sensibilities diminish, respiration and the action of the heart become more imperfect, and suffocation more urgent; but consciousness now fails to be roused to put forth a voluntary effort for relief; and the poor abused and languishing nerves, whose office it is to stand sentinel at the fountains of life, obtaining no help from the muscles of volition, at last are compelled quietly to yield up the struggle; and the person is found dead in his bed, the cause unknown."

Sometimes the victims of the weed end their days in all the horrors of *delirium tremens*, as was the case with Judge B—— C——, who was very active and efficient in all benevolent enterprises, and one of the main pillars of the Congregational church at T——. He made no use of alcoholic drink—was a distinguished friend of the Temperance Reformation, and made no use of tobacco, except for smoking, and for two or three years that was incessant. On his way to church he would smoke till he came to the meeting-house steps, and then light his pipe on the steps after service, and for the last few months of his life he shut himself in his room, and mourned and smoked without cessation.

A less mournful case was that of a Worthy Patriarch who was subject to *delirium tremens* by the use of tobacco. He had horrible writhings—strange visions—and objects of a hideous nature, well-nigh of every form and hue, harrowed up his soul and wrought upon his imagination. On the recurrence of one of these painful paroxysms, the doctor fixed his eye on the eye of the maniac, and the following passed between them:

"Do you use strong drinks?"

"No."

"Do you belong to the Sons of Temperance?"

"Yes."

"I supposed you did. You use tobacco. This is a tobacco fit—this is *delirium tremens*. You may die in the next one. Drop tobacco, or tobacco will drop you."

The former Worthy Patriarch dropped tobacco, and was cured.

It is the almost unanimous testimony of physicians, that the use of tobacco seriously aggravates many diseases, does NOT preserve from malaria or contagion, and by its depressing effect upon the vital forces, often renders diseases fatal that would otherwise be easily curable. Besides, we find laid down in medical books, EIGHTY-SEVEN diseases named as caused by its use, and physicians estimate that twenty thousand of our people are killed by it every year. It is for these reasons, doubtless, that prize-fighters, when under training, are not permitted to use it at all, because they cannot afford to risk a failure in the fearful struggle that taxes to the utmost every sustaining and recuperative energy, merely for the sake of a transient indulgence.

This point may now be deemed to be conclusively established, viz. : by the operation of the chemical and physiological laws involved in the use of tobacco, its invariable tendency is to induce disease in a healthy organism ; and therefore the tobacco habit falls under the ban of the first principle laid down in page 9, by which to determine the unjustifiableness of indulgence.

But let us press the inquiry a little further.

SECTION 2. Is the Tobacco Habit an indulgence which tends directly, and of natural consequence, to induce other habits of an injurious character?

Says Dr. Griscom ("The Use of Tobacco," p. 34) : "One of the most common and serious effects is the demand for alcoholic drinks to satisfy the extreme thirst, and obviate the prostration of the physical functions resulting from the high temperature and the narcotic influence of the burning weed. There is no doubt that a large amount of the intemperance now so prevalent, is the immediate and direct effect of tobacco-chewing and smoking, and no individual, however safe he may feel himself against intemperance before yielding to the temptation of tobacco-smoking, can rely upon himself to avoid it after considerable indulgence in the latter practice, as both his moral and intellectual sensibilities are almost certain to become impaired, *which fact he cannot himself appreciate.*

"It is therefore difficult and almost impossible for a confirmed lover of tobacco to avoid the terrible evils of intemperance."

There is so much truth in this quotation, that we hesitate to modify its force in the least. Yet facts compel the admission that the statement in the last paragraph is extreme. There are many "confirmed lovers of tobacco" who do *not* feel the "difficulty" named; yet, *the reason why they do not* is a complete confirmation of the correctness of Dr. Griscom's general position, viz.: that the use of tobacco tends toward indulgence in spirituous beverages; for the reason that they do not feel that difficulty we believe in every case to be this, viz: the excessive use of stimulants in some other form, such as tea, coffee, spices, etc.

Says Dr. Rush: "One of the usual effects of smoking and chewing, is thirst. This thirst cannot be allayed by water, for no sedative, or even insipid liquor, will be relished after the mouth and throat have been exposed to the stimulus of the smoke or the use of tobacco."

Says Dr. Mussey: "In the practice of smoking there is no small danger. It produces a huskiness of the mouth, which calls for some liquid. Water is too insipid, as the nerves of taste are in a half-palsied state, from the influence of tobacco-smoke; hence, in order to be tasted, an article of a pungent or stimulating character is resorted to, and hence, the kindred habits of smoking and drinking."

Says Dr. J. C. Jackson, pages 19–21: "Inquiry, on a very large scale, into the habits of men who have been known as habitual drinkers of alcoholic liquors, has settled the point conclusively that their appetites for strong drink were created and made clamorous by their previous use of tobacco, whose depressing effects upon their nervous systems were such as to establish an instinctive or impulsive desire for an offset.

"The chaplain of the State Prison at Auburn, N. Y., for the year 1854, I think, reports that out of over seven hundred male prisoners, six hundred were convicted of crime when under the direct or reflex influence of ardent spirits, and that a personal inquiry into the appetitial habits of this class of persons brought out this startling and forcible truth, that five-sixths, or five hundred out of six hundred who were convicted for crime when partially or ravingly drunk, had, from their own statements, the desire for strong drink awakened in them so clamorously as to demand gratification at any rate, by the depressing effects on their nervous systems of the use of tobacco. Outside of this statistical statement, my own investigations, in a much larger measure, go to corroborate the truth of this record. I have never yet known, in all my inquiries or researches, a single habitual user of alcoholic drinks who was not a tobacco chewer. I have heard of but one habitual drunkard who never used tobacco.

"Now, while it does not universally follow that every tobacco-chewer uses ardent spirits, it will be found uniformly to be the fact, that he does use some form of stimulant or excitant, as a substitute therefor. There are countervailing forces in operation in respect to the use of ardent spirits, such as the influence of public opinion against their use. A great many men and women, within the last thirty years, have had their moral sense very much exercised and educated in respect to the dangers arising from the habitual use of alcoholic liquors. But, while made sensible of the dangers in this respect, little or no instruction has been given in regard to the risks run from the use of intoxicating poisons of a different kind. Hence it will be found, upon close examination, that thousands of persons who have given up the use of alcoholic drinks, have substituted in their places table beverages, or intoxicating drugs, to make up for their loss of their old accustomed stimulant. In proof of this, statistics go to show that opium, outside of the use of it by the profession as a medicine, has increased in sale over 300 per cent. within the last twenty years. Lawyers, ministers, artists, doctors, students, men of letters, in many instances, are in the daily use of opium. Others who do not use it, have substituted for alcoholic beverages, hasheesh—extract of hemp—or absinthe—extract of wormwood, whilst others use the strongest effusions of tea and coffee, drinking these twice, at least, and very many of them three times a day, and along with these, using the most stimulating condiments upon their food, thus subjecting their nervous systems to such influence from the introduction of these stimuli and narcotic properties into their circulation as to make good, in large measure, for their total abstinence from alcoholic drinks. Thus related in their expressions of Nervous Force to the use of drinks and foods which serve in part as substitutes for alcoholic stimulants, they keep up their use of tobacco, and so demonstrate most manifestly the truth of the statement made above, that while every or nearly every user of alcoholic drinks does use tobacco, in some of its forms, and while tobacco users do not all use alcoholic drinks, they do all of them use, in some form or other, such substitutes for alcoholic drinks as their sense of moral propriety and their regard for their characters in the public esteem will permit."

Surely, after such testimony, it must be admitted that the tobacco habit does tend directly, and of natural consequence, to induce other habits of an injurious character, and is therefore condemned by the second principle laid down as a test of unjustifiable indulgence.

SECTION 3. Does the tobacco indulgence transmit to posterity diseased conditions and perverted tendencies?

"Writers who have investigated the subject are generally agreed that tobacco diminishes virility. There can be no doubt that such is its action on persons who commence the use of it early in life. We hold this to be a conclusive demonstration of the general rule, that the influence of tobacco on the human constitution is hurtful, for an agent which enervates the procreative power must exert a deleterious influence on the progeny." *Dr. Henry Gibbins*, p. 17.

"If the evil ended with the individual who, by the indulgence of a pernicious custom, injures his own health and impairs his faculties of mind and body, he might be left to his own enjoyment, his *fool's paradise*, unmolested. This, however, is not the case. *In no instance is the sin of the father more strikingly visited upon the children than the sin of tobacco-smoking*. The enervation, the hypochondriasis, the hysteria, the insanity, the dwarfish deformities, the consumption, the suffering lives and early death of the children of inveterate smokers, bear ample testimony to the feebleness and unsoundness of the constitution transmitted by this pernicious habit."

Says Dr. R. T..Trall (p. 14, "Tobacco"): "The habitual tobacco-user, in his propagating his kind, will inevitably curse his offspring with an organization more or less disordered, and a class of vital functions more or less unbalanced. That parent whose blood and secretions are saturated with tobacco, and whose brain and nervous system are constantly semi-narcotized by its influence, must transmit to the child so unfortunate as to be born unto him, the elements of a distempered body and an erratic mind, a deranged condition of organic atoms, which *invariably elevates the animalism of the future being, at the expense of the moral and intellectual nature.*"

That diseased conditions and perverted tendencies are transmitted by the tobacco habit, from parent to child, is thus established beyond question, and hence the indulgence, as such, is passed beyond the bar of justification by the third principle laid down as a touch-stone of right conduct.

4. Is it so strengthening to selfishness as to injure spiritual interests?

Mark, the question is not, Is it totally destructive of Christian character? but, Is it *injurious* to spiritual interests?

Let us first take its *expensiveness* as an index of the truth upon this point, proceeding upon the assumption that the character of one's stewardship will necessarily modify his whole religious character.

In 1852, Great Britain paid, in duties alone, upon tobacco, a sum equal to two dollars per head for her entire population. "New York city," says McGregor, "spends more each day for tobacco than for bread; *i.e.*, in the ratio of $10,000 to $8,500."

The United States and Great Britain could support 100,000 ministers of the gospel, at average rates, upon what they now spend for this single indulgence.

Many a young man in fashionable life pays more for this than for his board-bill. Many a mechanic will die, and leave his family without a cent, who pays more for this than the cost of a life assurance of two thousand dollars.

The American church, says Dr. Coles, consumes $5,000,000 in it every year.

The present annual production of tobacco has been estimated by an English writer at 4,000,000,000 pounds! This is smoked, chewed, and snuffed. Suppose it all made into cigars, one hundred to the pound, it would produce four hundred billions. Allowing this tobacco, unmanufactured, to cost ten cents a pound, and we have $400,000,000 expended every year. At least one and a-half times as much more is required to manufacture it into a marketable form and dispose of it to the consumer. If this be so, then the human family expend, every year, one thousand millions of dollars in the gratification of an acquired habit, or one dollar for every man, woman and child upon the earth!

This sum would build two railroads around the earth, at a cost of twenty thousand dollars per mile, or sixteen railroads from the Atlantic to the Pacific! It would build one hundred thousand churches, costing $10,000 each; or half a million school-houses, costing $2,000 each; or one million dwellings, costing $1,000 each! It would employ one million preachers and one million teachers, giving each a salary of $500. It would support three and one-third millions of young men at college, giving each $300 per annum for expenses.

No man, however prejudiced he may be in favor of tobacco, can deny that this immense waste is a huge sin against God's mercies, and a terrible blight upon the best interests of the race. In so far, therefore, as he participates in it, he necessarily strengthens the selfish propensities of his nature, and to a corresponding extent damages his spiritual interests.

But the proof upon this point is not merely or mainly inferential. Says a sensible writer:

"The question naturally occurs, How is it that such a destructive and expensive indulgence should ever prevail? I answer, Its animalizing and sensualizing power blots the purity of mental discernment. But for this, every man with light upon the subject would regard it as a mighty evil, at war with nature and human obligation; hostile to strict virtue and Christian self-denial; an indulgence unworthy the true dignity of man; a resource for happiness below the standard of the brute.

"In this way tobacco tramples on the dictates of enlightened reason, vetoes the decisions of the judgment, and paralyzes the strength of common sense. By saturating the whole brain with its narcotic oil, its pure normal action no longer exists; a morbid force is substituted; and the divinely-arranged beatitudes of the natural senses are prostituted to the grossest forms of sensuality.

"Send the victim of this habit to his daily avocation in his workshop, after forty-eight hours of suspension of its indulgence, and he cannot find his tools; or, finding them, does not know how to use them. Send him to the counting-room—he cannot perform a reckoning; he cannot make out his bills. Mind is so benumbed, it cannot act till goaded up by artificial forcings. The minister in the pulpit and the lawyer at the bar are wanting in zeal till quickened by the potency of tobacco! If the client get his case, or the minister preach with zeal, it is not by the native genius of brain, or the inspiration of the Spirit of God, but by the unhallowed excitement of gratified lust!"

Says Dr. Henry Gibbons (p. 28): "It will not be denied that the appetite for tobacco is entirely sensual and animal; that it is associated with the lowest grade of human influences; that it pertains to no endowment which man possesses in distinction from the beast. Therefore, it cultivates and strengthens the animal nature at the expense of the intellectual and moral. Its tendency is to degrade the higher qualities of our being."

Tyrrell testifies that it is one of those "pleasant vices" which the just gods make instruments to scourge us, and that it destroys the very principle of manhood.

An eminent English surgeon, as quoted by Dr. Gibbons (p. 21), writes: "I have invariably found that patients addicted to tobacco-smoking were in spirit cowardly, and deficient in manly fortitude to undergo any surgical operation."

Says Dr. Solly, of St. Thomas's Hospital: "I believe, if the habit of smoking advances in England as it has done for the last ten years, that the English character will lose that combination of energy and solidity that has hitherto distinguished it, and that England will fall in the scale of nations." Quoted by Dr. Elam, page 121, "A Physician's Problems."

The philosophy of the matter is thus clearly stated by Dr. J. C. Jackson ("Tobacco," p. 39):

"Pathological investigations go to show that different poisons show different effects upon the nervous system; that different portions of the brain are affected by different poisons; and that corresponding difference in mental and moral conditions, under the administrations of different poisons, are exhibited.

"Alcohol, for instance, in producing abnormal conditions of the responsible faculties, specifically affects those which we describe as intellectual; while narcotics—as tobacco, for instance—affect those which are usually described as moral faculties. Watch closely the changes of character through which persons respectively pass as their vital forces come to act on these respective poisons, and it will be seen that while alcohol disturbs those departments of the brain through which the intellectual faculties find manifestion, tobacco affects those portions of the brain through which the moral sensibilities normally express themselves.

"Drunkards, unless when in a state of decided insensibility or wild delirium, retain their moral sense, when compared with their loss of judgment, most remarkably. In truth, if but partially intoxicated, their moral forces seem to be quickened and excited, while their reasoning powers are in a great state of perturbation. The tobacco-user, however, finds himself in such relations to the use of his higher faculties as not to have his reason particularly disturbed. You see men on the street, in their studies, in public and private intercourse, who are users of tobacco, who show no less intellectual shrewdness or profundity, where the intellect takes cognition of subjects that are mainly within the province of the reason, than they would if they did not use it; but the moment that they pass that line, and step into the department of the affections or the higher emotions, or proceed to the examination of questions which for a right decision depend upon large spiritual discrimination, they exhibit a degree of abnormality indicative of decided obtuseness or positive aberration."

The progress of deterioration is thus described, p. 41: "From the first day of the year to the last he is under immoral conditions. The Passional Forces, or those that find their point of efficient action at the base of his brain, are uppermost in him. The Moral Forces, or those which work themselves up into vigor through the action of that portion of the brain which is mapped out by the coronal region, are benumbed, or nearly dead. Gradually the Manly and Divine die out of him, steadily the Beastly develops itself in him, till at length those sentiments and affections, impulses and inspirations, which are well described as the Intuitive Forces of his nature, go into the shadow, and have no directing power in the shaping of his life or the exhibitions of his conduct. At length, though naturally endowed with more than ordinary intimate relations to the True, the Noble and the Good, he becomes intimately associated with the False, the Ignoble and the Mean, and unless vicarious effort is made for him he is a lost man."

Not many years ago the Council of

Berne, in Switzerland, recognized the principle here stated by prohibiting tobacco to all youths under fifteen years of age. More recently the French Minister of Public Instruction, after classifying the pupils of a college into smokers and non-smokers, finding the latter to be the best students, and that this was the fact elsewhere, prohibited the use of tobacco in all the colleges of France.

A habit that prodigally wastes large sums of money, weakens the intellect, and subordinates the moral nature to the sensual, must plead guilty to this last count in the indictment against indulgences; it does strengthen the selfish principles of the nature to the detriment of the spiritual interests.

Now, can that which is so obviously WRONG in the aggregate, be right in the individual?

We have seen that its use must tend toward disease by the chemical and physiological laws brought into play; that it leads directly and by natural consequence to habits of an injurious character; that it transmits diseased conditions to posterity, and that it is strengthening to selfishness and demoralizing to the mind. Hence this habit meets the unsparing condemnation of all the principles laid down on page 10 as prohibiting indulgence, and therefore can only be justified by the individual, if at all, upon the ground of some physiological reason that transports it at once from the field of either preferred or constrained indulgence into the region of remedial agency to be employed only as scientifically directed.

Its use, however, is excused by Dr. Elam, in "A Physician's Problems," pp. 122 and 123, after this manner:

"On the other hand many men of high scientific attainments and sound judgment consider the use of tobacco in moderation, and especially under certain circumstances of great hardship and privation; as soldiers when in active service, for instance, as not only not injurious, but beneficial, both hygienically, therapeutically, and psychically; whilst in common with their opponents, they recognize freely the very deleterious consequences attendant upon its abuse manifested particularly in various nervous lesions which eminently indicate degeneration. It is probable that were society in a more natural condition, or one more in accordance with the most obvious rules of hygiene, no poisonous agent, narcotic or stimulant, would be habitually desirable or allowable. But want and misery, unhealthy dwellings and occupations, the rapid whirl and contest of life, the wear and tear of hand work and brain work; rivalry, emulation, anxiety, and all the corroding passions and affections, with the thousand irregularities that help to form the sum of modern existence; all these constitute for society what may fairly be called a diseased state, which may properly be counteracted by narcotics in some form. It may be that they are producing various forms of ill, but we do not know quite certainly what they may prevent, nor what strange new nervous phenomena might be manifested if we should attempt to put 'new wine into old bottles,' by adopting a rigorously simple regimen, freed from all stimulants and narcotics, to so clearly unnatural a mode of life as the mass of men now lead.

"The urgent need which all people appear to feel for these agents in some form, the craving after and the determination to have them at whatever price, seem to me to indicate something more than a mere moral dereliction and to point out some stern necessity in the constitution of men or society, which may not be gainsaid.

"Amid all the evils, too, which arise from the abuse of alcoholic liquids and tobacco, and they are proteiform, we are not without grounds of consolation. Perhaps there are few nations of Europe where certain classes of the population drink more habitually, and smoke more constantly than in England; yet the rate of mortality is lower in England than in any other European nation, although it is to be feared that this rate is slowly increasing; but mass for mass, or man for man, it is readily acknowledged that no people can compete with our own, whether for energy, or endurance, or bodily labor."

Here are five arguments, the first of

which, based upon the opinions of some scientific men, is more than answered by recalling the fact that the great majority of such men hold opinions directly the *reverse* of that expressed by Dr. Elam.

The second argument from the diseased condition of society finds a sufficient answer in this: Many who have deemed themselves under the strongest necessity to use it, have, under christian influences, discontinued its use, and *always with decided advantage to health,* no matter how imperative, or long continued the habit may have been; hence the doctor's hypothesis concerning the remedy needed is opposed by *facts*, and becomes void.

The third argument from the almost universal craving of the people for narcotics is not sound; for the premise may be admitted while the conclusion not only does not, but ought not to follow.

The craving indicates diseased conditions, like the hunger of dyspeptic stomachs, and the only "constitutional necessity" in the case, is the necessity for *restorative treatment,* which certainly does *not* consist in pampering the disease.

The fourth argument, from the habits of certain classes of the English people, is given a broader application than facts will justify, for England's enterprise and low death-rate are *not* dependent upon those particular classes. Those classes exhibit precisely the opposite state of facts, while her favorable climate, the comparative freedom of the masses of the population from worse vices, the skill of her physicians, and other circumstances, such as the diffusion of intelligence, etc. sufficiently account for the low rate of mortality and the abounding energy of the people.

In the fifth argument the good doctor's attempt to neutralize the damaging force of the *ill effects* of the tobacco habit, by the assumption that we "do not know what they may prevent" is simply ridiculous. Suppose the same argument were used in support of gambling; we do not know but it may prevent highway robbery, therefore the "rigorous regimen" of honesty should not be applied in this direction. Would this be satisfactory? Yet the argument is just as good in one case as in the other. We conclude, therefore, that this attempt to justify the habit is an utter failure.

If, then, it ought to be abandoned, the question, *How?* becomes one of vital importance.

The difficulty of the undertaking few can realize before making the effort.

Says Dr. Jackson ("Tobacco," p. 7): "Just to the degree that a vice has for its existence no other justification than the indulgence of mere animal propensity, and is therefore beyond the pale of reason, is it difficult to reach and overthrow it, provided always that it has secured to itself such general assent as to place before it for its protection the social forces, and to make it fashionable. I know this was true in my own case when trying to abandon the use of tobacco."

How then shall the foe be throttled? Dr. Trall answers ("Prize Essay, Tobacco," p. 21): "Let the man resume, for the occasion, his whole manhood, and, following the memorable example of one who deserved to be free and independent in relation to another form of slavery, declare, 'Live or die, survive or perish, I am for no more tobacco,' and he will almost surely triumph. The struggle may be terrible, but it will be brief. He may feel like death, but he will not die. In a week or two the severest ordeal may be passed; and, in a month or two, the morbid love may be changed to a healthful hate. The sufferer must determine to be free indeed, with full and unreserved purpose of soul; nor must he seek substitutes of any kind."

Dr. Joel Shaw answers ("Tobacco," p. 113): "Put the foot of moral determination upon the head of the serpent Passion, and cast him out forever from you, and in a few days your triumph will be achieved."

All this is doubtless good, but Dr. Jackson reveals a better way, and both for warning and encouragement we quote a portion of his experience, pp. 14 to 16:

"After having been married some few weeks I was rudely awakened from my silly and foolish dream-life to a consciousness that no slave was ever more thoroughly fettered than I was. My wife said to me, 'I wish you could find it compatible with your ideas of propriety to give up the use of tobacco. Your breath is offensive to me.' Instanter I said, 'I will give it up. Nothing will afford me greater delight than to yield to your request. I will never use any more of it.' So I entered upon my renunciation, and in twenty-four hours was as thoroughly conscious of my enslavement as any one could be. Oh, how my nervous system suffered from the want of its daily draught of poison. The most violent headache and blindness, equal to that which was induced when I first indulged in the use of tobacco, came upon me, and such complete prostration of my physical powers, and depression of mind, with peturbation of spirit, I hope never during my mortal life to be called upon again to endure. My blood played through my veins as if it were in a sea-surge. I saw all invisible things that were ugly and demon-like,—devils in the shape of old women, haggish and witch-like, danced around me. For the first time in my life I became sensible of the *enslaving* power of appetite. No force of will, or vigor of conscience were competent to my deliverance. My love for my wife, which usually absorbed all my self, faded away into nothingness. I saw nothing, thought of nothing, felt nothing but the overpowering desire for my tobacco. My moral sense became inert, and like a dog to his vomit, or a sow to her wallowing in the mire, I laid my manhood down, and for the time being was transformed into a beast. When, however, I had re-induced the habitual conditions of the nervous system by a return to my chewing and smoking, then came up more vividly than ever my loss of self-respect. A young and newly married man, I saw that 'to will was present with me, but how to do good I found not.' A Christian by profession, I felt ashamed, and resolved to break the appetite. For the better part of three months I repeatedly made efforts for my deliverance, and each time fell into deeper disgrace than before. Ultimately my nature became so thoroughly demoralized by *vain* attempts to recover its dignity and poise, that the baser and meaner elements in it were uppermost, and, for a time, there are no words in the English language which so decidedly describe the impression I had of myself, as when I say that I had become a thorough Sneak.

Out of this deep of degradation I found no earthly hand to lift me. My wife I could not appeal to; for my very impotency had become my infamy. So there was no help in that direction. No friends came to my aid. Everybody around me was using tobacco. At length—and I scarcely know how it came to pass—I bethought me of the Saviour. I remembered what the apostle James said, 'If any man lack wisdom, let him ask of God, who giveth to every man liberally, and upbraideth not.' I was about to leave home on a journey. Beseeching the Saviour to help me recover my lost character, I went out in the darkness. I knew the nature of the conflict, and scarcely believed that I should succeed; but there came to me angels that strengthened me; and from that hour to this, the poison has not passed my lips. For four months, however, I was in a wild and dreamy haze, staggering through mist and darkness; a dozen times a day tempted and well nigh overborne, but conquering for the hour and struggling on."

But we proclaim a BETTER WAY THAN THAT!—a way by which even the unfortunate subject of the following sketch might have been saved. Again we quote from "Tobacco and Its Effects," by Dr. J. C. Jackson:

"Early in my professional practice, I was visited by a clergyman who wished to place himself under my care, with a view to be relieved of diseases with which he was afflicted; and, upon examination of his case, I said to him that I thought he could not be cured—that his nervous system had become so deranged by infiltration of some poison into his blood that I feared his constitutional power to react under its disuse would fail him. * * * * When he came to consult me he was about fifty years of age. He first became alarmed in regard to its effect upon him, after having had an interview with a brother clergyman, in respect to the propriety of organizing a simultaneous movement on the part of all the clergymen in the city where he resided by preaching against the use of tobacco. When requested by his clerical brother to unite in such a movement, he distinctly declined. When asked why, his reply was, that he did not believe in preaching against sin of which he himself was guilty. When still farther questioned why he did not abandon the sin, his answer was that he was unable to do it. When his brother almost indignantly inquired if he, a Christian minister, felt himself at liberty to say that he was guilty of a sin of which he could not repent, he replied in the affirmative. To show his inability, he then related the following circumstance:

"For a month previous to this interview, his mind had been greatly impressed with his sin and his shame in this matter of the use of tobacco, and he had sought privately to abandon it. On the Sabbath preceding the visit of his clerical friend he had determined to enter the pulpit free from his usual indulgence. On arising to open the church services he found himself blind, and his organs of articulation paralyzed so that he could not utter a word. He came very near falling down in a fit. Some of the members of his congregation, seeing that he was sick, took him home, services being dispensed with, and a physician immediately attended him. Asking all the persons who were around him to leave him alone with the physician, who was scarcely less frightened than they, he said to him, 'My friend, you need not be at all troubled. Just hand me my tobacco-box that lies in the pigeon-hole in my book case, and I shall be all right in two minutes. This is simply a reaction of my nervous system consequent upon abstinence from my usual indulgences.'

"The physician gave him his tobacco; he took a chew, and was in fifteen minutes as well as he ever was—so well, that in the afternoon the services were continued. The feeling of mortification that came over him when he found that his whole intellectual and moral nature was enslaved by a physical habit, he told me he had no language to describe; and then and there he made me promise as a physician, and as a Christian gentleman, pledge myself to be faithful, in season and out of season, in my rebukes and reproofs of the use of tobacco—saying, that though he had himself become the victim of it, and for many years during his use of it had had no idea that he was doing wrong thereby, within the last month he had felt that there was no evil in our entire land, not excepting that of the habitual use of intoxicating liquors, so much to be deplored and so thoroughly to be dreaded in its effects upon our youth as the habit of chewing and smoking tobacco.

"A few weeks after this interview he died. A post mortem examination was held. No evidences of diseased structure were exhibited in any of the internal organs except the heart. When the operators reached the heart and took it out, they found it nearly disorganized. The tenacious coherence of its fibres had entirely disappeared, and one of the physicians present at the examination wrote me that it could be 'picked to pieces with as much ease as a piece of fried liver.'"

INSTANTANEOUS EXTIRPATION, by the *power of grace*, in answer to prayer, is the BEST WAY!!

But, is it possible? Let testimony decide.

In "The Christian Advocate and Journal" of July 31, 1873, the Author published a series of questions, the third one of which read as follows:

"Can men be *instantaneously* delivered from the power of acquired habits, such as the use of tobacco, rum, etc., so that they shall thereafter have no craving for the indulgence?"

The first reply that we insert is from an esteemed minister, widely known in official relations other than professional:

"I have been an habitual smoker of tobacco for more than thirty years. There have been brief periods during which I abstained from its use; but the power of the habit was so great, that I yielded to the craving of my appetite, and in each instance became a more inveterate smoker than before. During the last three or four years, I have had many troublesome thoughts in regard to the practice, for I was trying to be wholly the Lord's.

"A little more than three months ago, I deliberately laid my pipe aside, after enjoying an evening's smoke, with a clear and well-defined conviction that it was the last time that I should thus indulge a habit that had become absolutely tyrannical. I made no promise, as I had done on previous occasions; but I felt, through my whole moral and religious self, that the decision had been reached. For a moment I felt almost a terror as I remembered former times of attempted reform, and the ghosts of broken promises came trooping before my mental vision. But I trusted in the Lord, and not one word of his precious promises has failed me. Once, after the lapse of a fortnight, the simple thought, 'I'd like to smoke,' came to my mind; but no sooner was it formed than it disappeared. I have had no craving, no uneasiness, no desire. I simply wonder at the folly that ruled me so long, and praise God for a victory as complete as instantaneous."

As some time has elapsed since the above was written, further information was asked and received, in the following notes:

October 16, 1873.

Rev. Bro. :—Be so kind as to inform me whether longer time has made any new developments in your experience of abstinence from tobacco, and oblige,

Yours Fraternally,

S. H. PLATT.

REPLY.

October 17, 1873.

Dear Bro. :—It gives me much pleasure to say that, *through grace*, I can emphasize all I said before. I know of no language too strong to express either the completeness of the victory or the extent of my gratitude to God for so signal a blessing. Yours Fraternally,

—— ——.

Still later, in answer to further inquiries, comes the following note:

Rev. S. H. PLATT. Dear Brother:—A little more than a year has elapsed since I left off the use of tobacco—an account of which I gave you, perhaps seven months ago. This further time has more fully developed the thoroughness of the cure then spoken of, and the completeness of the victory over an evil habit. I am filled with wonder, for I expected a terrible fight with an appetite strengthened by an indulgence of about thirty-five years; but the enemy has not showed his head. Not only has the desire for smoking been effectually squelched, but a perfect hatred of smoking has been developed, on account of the offensiveness of the odor of tobacco. I frequently cross a street, or change my seat in a car, to escape the puff of smoke, or the fœtid breath of a smoker. Yet I have no hard words for my brethren who are enslaved. My great deliverance has mellowed my entire soul, and I can sympathize deeply with those who are in bondage. "Thanks be unto God, who giveth us the victory."

      Yours Fraternally,

The next is from a lady thus vouched for by the editor of "The Home Altar," to whom we are indebted for the experience: "She is one of my patrons—a woman who has power with God in prayer."

"When quite young I was advised to use tobacco for my eyes. The prescription was made an excuse for the practice. After my conversion I was enabled to see the inconsistency of such useless habits with gospel requirements. I would sometimes lay it aside, thinking never to touch it again, but, true to nature, would soon resume its use.

"In the course of my 'steppings heavenward,' the necessity of holiness of heart and life were made plain to me, principally through the medium of Mrs. Palmer's works.

"While meditating upon the subject and counting the cost, this same habit was brought under consideration. I knew how much I loved the narcotic weed; it rested me when weary, soothed me when sad or in trouble. Having read my Bible much, I could at once turn to any portion that I thought might have any bearing upon the point in question.

"The most careful and prayerful research only left it for conscience to decide. In my consecration I rested the matter thus: 'O Lord, if at any future time I am made to see this habit contrary to *thy will*, relying upon *thy strength I will give it up.*' The Spirit at once assured my heart that was sufficient. Some eight months after I had received the blessing of perfect love, while pleading that one *dear* to me might be strengthened to give up intoxicating drinks, the question, with much force, was presented: 'Is it consistent to plead thus, while you are guilty of a practice equally useless?' I tried to think it satanic influence seeking to ensnare me, but it was impossible to evade the matter; I had to honestly face it, and in loving obedience, the idol was placed upon the altar of sacrifice. From that moment the appetite was gone; when friends would insist that I should use it, a feeling of aversion for the habit would arise in my heart.

"In after life, having lost the direct witness, or that sacred nearness to Jesus, when the gentle insinuation was made that tobacco might help my failing sight, my *mind consented*, and immediately my love for its use returned.

"After indulging the habit for some months, my conscience smote me, and thinking to lay it aside, I found that *will, resolutions* and *vows* were all inadequate to oust the enemy; its strength was doubled. Never before did I have one feeling of pity or sympathy for noble, godlike manhood bound hand and foot by the demon fetters of intemperance. I learned from experience there was but one way of deliverance. I went to my closet and with strong crying and tears, and many prayers, told Jesus. I asked him to remove the appetite. The gracious answer came immediately."

The following is from a minister in the West:

Rev. S. H. PLATT. Dear Sir:—Yours of Sept. 18 remains unanswered. I will now reply. As respects question 3d: A physician of extended practice was converted or reclaimed while I had charge of the place in which he lived. He had acquired the habit of using large quantities of whisky and brandy, together with tobacco, and withal more or less given to licentiousness. Since that time he has been steadily advancing in morals and moral power, till he now preaches the gospel as a local preacher, side by side with the best of the district. "Was it instantaneous?" Yes, as respects tobacco; he became convicted of its sinfulness by a voice saying, "That is not the way to glorify God. Stop, and stop now!" And from that moment, he says, he has never used it, neither does he in any way like the smell, or even the sight of tobacco.

As to myself, I had used it from childhood, and the love and use thereof grew upon me. I became convicted of its sinfulness, went to God and said, "Destroy the appetite, or give me power over it. Save me, that I may glorify Thee as a God of power for our present sins, and I will glorify Thee evermore." I wrote out the contract, and signed it, and from that blessed afternoon until to-day, have no recollection of ever desiring it even ; and, what is still more convincing, is this qualifying fact, that when I have taken back the consecration through other avenues, as by neglect of other duties, coldness, or a departure from God, which I recall only a few times during my christian experience, there came with them the old *desire* for tobacco—it tasted good. With the light of returning day came the power that silenced the demand.

———— ————.

Here follows one from a private christian in Vermont :

"Soon after my conversion I was chosen President of the Young People's Christian Association, and attended three religious meetings every week; so you see that tobacco was a great trouble to me ; and I had tried a number of times to leave it off, but could not do so.

"One night as I was retiring to rest I thought I would kneel by my bed and ask Him who never refuses to answer prayer, to take from me the desire for tobacco, and from that moment it has been impossible for me to use it."

An editor in Tennessee writes thus:

September 25, 1873.

Dear Sir:—In response to your call for testimony in reference to the ability to break off from the habit of using tobacco, in answer to prayer, I will say that I smoked tobacco excessively for fifteen years, commencing when I was about twenty years old, having used it more or less for several years previously. I ever found that the use of it was injurious to both my nervous system and my religious enjoyments. I cannot say that at that time I felt under condemnation in the use of it, as I would now, with the increase of spiritual light and life I now enjoy over and above what I did then; but the *luxury* of it always affected my religious enjoyments, and I often strove to break off from the use of it; indeed I determined time and again to desist from it, sometimes abstaining for a few months or weeks, once for twelve months; *but the desire for it never left me*, and whenever

I tasted it I was sure to take to it again. I sometimes vowed while upon my knees in prayer, to abstain from it and never touch it again, but I always attempted to do this in my own strength—hence I failed, being overcome by the almost irresistible influence it had upon my appetite so long cultivated to the use. This marked the period of nearly fifteen years of my using it.

One Sunday morning, the first day of December, 1850, I retired to a secluded place, got down upon my knees and asked the Lord to help me quit it, determining then and there that I would, God being my helper, never touch the accursed thing again by any kind of use in the way of consumption, and from that day to this I have never had any desire to smoke or chew tobacco or to use it in any way; but I did this whenever I saw tobacco; I lifted my heart to God imploring his assistance in abstaining from it, I have now been clear of the desire of it for nearly twenty-three years.

Very respectfully,

A prominent business man in an inland city testifies:

"I used tobacco and it used to prevent me some times from getting a blessing, and I would fear that I yet would miss of heaven. I would weep, pray, and fast, but, as I thought, to no purpose; but God, who was leading me, knew better. That was the way my will had to be subdued, and my blessed Jesus knew how to do it. I often tried to abstain from tobacco, but as often failed, until God showed plainly that it was sin to use it because it was undermining my constitution. I murmured because my brethren could use it; why not I?—but that was nothing to me. 'Follow thou me' was the response, until I found if I would be the Lord's I must give it up with the rest of my idols; I concluded to do so; I loved my pipe as dearly as any one, but I laid it on the shelf and bid it farewell. I would use it no more. Turning to the Lord for strength to enable me to overcome, and to remove the appetite, I knew he could, but my faith was not strong enough to believe fully;

but I gave it up. Thirty-three years in forming the appetite, it was no easy matter; but to my surprise, as soon as I fully determined to give it up, all desire for it was gone. It was no hardship as I supposed it would be to overcome. How sweetly Jesus took the desire for it away. To Jesus be all the glory."

Now comes the story of a good old lady seventy-five years of age, written in her own quaint style, and rejoicing in a freedom of more than half a century:

"My mother used tobacco, had some trouble to get all she wanted. When I was a little child I practiced smoking secretly; when I was fourteen I experienced religion and thought I had ought to leave it, but did not. The next year or two after, sister Mary talked so good to me, I promised to the Lord in secret I would not smoke for a month. I kept my promise and did not smoke for a year and a half, then I tasted it again and wanted it as bad or worse than ever; then I indulged myself with it one and a half year, believing I could make a promise and be rid of it forever; so I made a secret promise to God, strong as I could. Like Nehemiah, I shook my lap and said, 'So let God shake me out of his favor if I do not keep this promise.' I did not keep it one day, and I don't know as I could; then I despaired till my brother said my sin was not unpardonable; then I wept seven days and seven nights. Like David, I made my bed to swim with tears because I was bound to that filthy, shameful habit. I was then twenty-one, thought I could appear well enough if it was not for that. After this I prayed, and God showed me that my heart was full of pride; then I had three weeks of painful seeking and striving to draw near to God; he made me smoke no more secretly; I must not be hypocritical. Then this good sister Mary and another brother did bear hard on me that I should leave it, or that I should break up the habit. I told them the whole, and said I could not, which made them harder yet toward me. I read to them the nineteenth chapter of Job, then I said, 'Let thy kingdom, blessed saviour, come and bid our jarring cease.' That instant it came in my mind that Jesus could take away all that wanting to smoke. I prayed that he might, and clapped my hands and said he would! Then they both thought they had been too hard with me. If they had said 'Hold on, you will get the victory,' I should never have wanted it again. Instead of that, Mary told me I might smoke, and I did not wait to know if it was gone. Then I wondered how I could ask, believing, and it not be done. A while after, I obtained the blessing of perfect love. The next sacrament, I asked that it might never defile my mouth again nor hinder my thoughts from serving God. From that time I have had no desire for it, and the smell of it is very disagreeable. This was at a quarterly meeting at Vermont, in 1821, January."

We now introduce a double cure which is thus narrated :

Nov. 20, 1873.

In answer to a card I saw in the "Methodist Home Journal," dated Aug.

16th, I will give you my experience in regard to acquired habits such as tobacco and rum. I am now forty-two years old; at the age of twelve years I commenced to use tobacco and continued to use it both smoking and chewing, till five years ago, when, in answer to prayer the appetite was instantly removed. The circumstances were as follows: I had tried many times to leave off the use of tobacco but the appetite was so strong that I could not withstand it. At one time I left it off for a month but not a day passed but I craved it, and when I did begin again it tasted as good as ever. I found the tobacco was injuring my health. My nervous system was very much deranged. For more than a year before I left it off there was scarcely a night but I lay for two or three hours before I could go to sleep. I resolved a great many times I would leave it off, but always failed. I had also acquired the habit of drinking and become a confirmed drunkard. I knew the habits were killing me, but I was powerless to stop. One evening a prayer meeting was appointed at my house; the minister (Elder Heath) in his remarks spoke about habits, and said that religion would cure all bad habits, such as tobacco, etc., and that by prayer God would remove evil appetites. I thought but little about it that night; was very careless and trifling about it. The next morning I took out my tobacco to take a chew, and thought of what the minister had said the night before. It was a new idea to me. I put the tobacco in my pocket again and said, I'll try it. I was alone in my barn; I kneeled down and asked God to remove the appetite from me. It was done. Glory to God! I was cured, I felt it, I knew it then, I have never had a desire for it since. There has been no hankering for it or for strong drink since. My sins were all forgiven and I was made a new man all over inside and outside. When I go into company where they are smoking I have no desire for it at all, neither have I for drinking, any more than if I had never had those habits. My nervous difficulty was instantly cured. No more trouble about sleeping, and I know that

Jesus can heal and remove and destroy all evil habits.

Another says: "I was a rum drinker when I gave my heart to Jesus, and when he gave me the evidence of my sins forgiven, away went the desire for rum. I was a tobacco-chewer and smoker and had been for thirty-five years. About two months after my conversion, it seemed as if this tobacco was to me a cherished habit, and I was thinking as Jesus had been so good to me to forgive me of all the past, what was I willing to give up for him in return, and the suggestion came to me, are you willing to give up the use of tobacco, either chewing or smoking, and I was enabled to answer yes, and then and there I was delivered from the desire or further craving for the indulgence, and so Jesus has kept me for about two years, and so I find him able to keep all we commit unto him."

The following is from an aged son of toil whose personal worth gives special emphasis to his words:

October, 1873.

Brother Platt:—You have called on me for a statement of my experience on tobacco. I smoked and chewed tobacco from a boy until thirty-eight years old, and also used intoxicating drinks the same length of time until both became strong habits. I was convinced it was a sin. My children were growing up around me, and I felt it wrong to set such examples. I promised to leave them off, but I felt my weakness, and called on my Heavenly Father, and told Him the work was too great for me, and prayed that he would do the work for me, and take away the taste or appetite. This was between 11 and 12 o'clock in the day time in the shop where I worked. I went home, ate my dinner, and laid my tobacco box on the shelf. My wife called to me to take my box, thinking that I had forgotten it. I said 'Let it be there,' and went out, trusting in the Lord. He heard my prayer. I never have had a taste or desire for a glass of intoxicating drink or a smoke or chew of tobacco from that time until the present moment, which is nineteen years the seventh of last February. Oh, I feel to thank God to-night while I pen this truth for the first time, for so great a deliverance! I feel I would do anything, deny myself of anything by the help of my God, for such a great deliverance for his children!

Here follows a sailor's experience:

October 27, 1873.

Dear Sir:—My testimony is this, that God saves me, and keeps me clean. I had used tobacco from the time of twelve years until I was forty-five years of age, and most of the time for thirty years, two pounds a week smoked and chewed. I was a sailor for thirty years, twenty-five years a member of a church. In 1870 I commenced to stop using tobacco, but could not. I then went to God in the middle of the street, the pipe burning in my mouth, and, blessed be His name, He delivered me. The appetite was totally lost, at once?

Yours respectfully,

Another sailor, now a member of the N. Y. E. Conference, thus writes:

November 27, 1873.

Dear Bro. Platt:—On Friday evening, Feb. 23, 1866, about 8 o'clock, I knelt at the altar rail in the lecture-room of the Alanson M. E. Church, Norfolk street, New York, *sick of sin*, a seeker of deliverance from the power and condemnation of the same. I was, at the time, a confirmed smoker, using the pipe when at sea to such an extent that it was a common occurrence for me to turn into my bunk with my pipe in my mouth. It was my inseparable companion during my night watches. When I gave up the sea, the desire for tobacco increased; it was growing with my growth, and strengthening with my strength. It was one of my idols. It is also worthy of remark that I had no *conviction*, either before or while at the altar, on the subject of tobacco—I had not looked upon it as a sin; but my consecration at that altar meant this, "I agree, from this time forth and *forever*, in the strength grace alone can supply, to renounce all manner of evil, to do, as far as in me lies, all manner of good; and being ignorant, and yet willing to be taught, I agreed to walk according to the light I had, was about to, and might ever after receive; and while thus kneeling, with such a consecration, I passed from death unto life. I became indeed a new creature in Christ Jesus. O the joy! O the peace! O the loathing of sin and all uncleanness. After meeting was closed I returned home. My family had all retired. The first object that caught my attention was my pipe. From mere force of habit, mechanically I took it down and attempted to smoke. I was sitting, meditating upon the strange and blissful experiences of the evening, when, lo! the appetite was GONE! Indeed, the pipe was positively distasteful to me. During the first week I made several attempts to smoke (intending, when my tobacco was used up to give up its use); every time the operation was distasteful; every time it brought condemnation. From that time to this I have neither used nor craved tobacco, and it requires about all the grace I can command to concede christian consistency to that man who acquires the habit after his conversion, or who persists in its continuance after he has acknowledged that the habit is one to be deplored, pernicious in its effects on the body always—too often on the soul. Of course the fact that God took away the appetite was sufficient reason to me not to resume its use; but there were other reasons which presented themselves to my mind at the time which were not without their influence. First, tobacco is not negative in its effects; it is either positive for good or evil. My experience attested to the latter. "Know ye not that ye are the temple of God, and that the spirit of God dwelleth in you? If any man defile the temple of God, him will God destroy." Second, I was a poor man, and would be robbing the cause of Christ of just so much money that might be used to further the benevolent enterprises of the Church. Third, I would be robbing my family by taking money that might be applied for their comfort, to pamper a depraved appetite. Also, as a Sabbath-school teacher, and an altar-worker in prayer-meetings, my influence for good would be marred just in proportion as I was not unlike the world. I have no craving for tobacco whatever.

Fraternally,
——— ———.

We conclude this Section by quoting from Rev. W. H. Boole's Tract: "Wonders of Grace," pp. 6-9, 1st ed. :

"I propose to relate a few of the numerous examples known to the writer, which have occurred under his personal observation, bearing directly upon this important point, and which demonstrate the power of divine grace in destroying sinful habits and appetites.

"A— C— has been for thirty years a member of the M. E. Church; for the greater part of this time a leader and trustee in a New York Church. His profession was always marked by correctness of deportment and generous zeal, whilst his cheerful manners won the esteem of all. But he had been addicted to the constant use of tobacco for forty years, until its daily use had become seemingly necessary to health, if not to life. He had made many efforts to rid himself of the doubtful practice, but always failed because of the inward gnawing which its long-continued use had created, and which forced him to begin the practice again. At last, on a certain occasion, in the presence of the writer, he said, 'I have long been seeking a deeper work of grace: tobacco appears to hinder me; but I had not supposed it possible to be saved from the dreadful power of this habit until now. Never before have I trusted Jesus to save me from the appetite as well as the use of it, but now I do;' and, suiting the action to the word, he threw far away from him the tobacco he held in his hand. He still lives, and for several years has reiterated this testimony: 'From that hour all desire left me, and I have ever since hated what I once so fondly loved.'

—— —— is a prominent member of the M. E. Church in the city of Brooklyn, N. Y. For thirty-five years he has served the church, giving liberally of his abundant means, and generally ready for every good word and work. From the age of ten he had used tobacco, until the habit had become so deeply rooted he could not endure to be without a cigar in his mouth, frequently rising in the night to "have a good smoke." During the thirty years of this manner of life, he often felt the bondage of the habit, and resolved against it, but his resolutions invariably failed him. About three years since, he became deeply interested in the subject of full salvation, and began diligently seeking for its possession. While pondering what might be the difficulties in his way, he saw that this very slavish habit was a bar to his advancement; but so earnest was he for the prize of a clean heart, that he felt altogether willing to yield up the indulgence, if it were possible. But was it? He had fought against the passion long and well, yet not once had he conquered. Who would deliver him from the body of this death? It was a new idea to him that Jesus saves from the appetite and lust of sin as well as from the act; that he gives grace not only to strive against, but to destroy the power of habit. But no sooner did he apprehend this gospel-truth, and read his privilege in the wonderful promise which stands at the head of this article, than he, all alone, one evening, cast himself on Jesus' word, and trusted him to do it for him. 'Twas done. Not an hour longer did the desire remain ; and his uniform testimony has ever since been : ''Tis strange to me that I ever loved the filthy practice.'

"These are not exceptional cases. They do not belong exclusively to men of 'peculiar temperament.' More than a score of examples equally interesting as those cited I have witnessed in one year, all occurring in the same community. Nor were these confined to Christians inquiring for the higher life of the full assurance of faith. Converts of a day have renounced the use of tobacco, trusting in Jesus for immediate salvation from the baneful craving, and received according to their faith."

Section 2.—The Opiate Habit.

This is so universally admitted to be wrong, that we will not occupy space in discussing the propriety of its indulgence. We quote again from "Wonders of Grace" pp. 9-11:

"Near the town of Westbrook, Conn., there lived an aged woman, seventy-two years old, well known in the community as the 'old opium eater,' who had lived in the daily use of large quantities of this drug for more than twenty-two years. Her daily allowance was enough to destroy the lives of twenty persons. Whether she ever had made any previous attempts to break away from the baneful practice, we know not; but, on a certain day, the writer visited her in company with a brother minister stationed in the town. The subject of her opium eating was introduced, and a close and faithful discussion on the moral aspects of the case followed. The *sin* of the habit was clearly and unhesitatingly exposed, and her unsaved and perilous condition, so far advanced in years, boldly but gently pronounced. Then Christ was presented, able to save to the uttermost—to save from the guilt and the passion of her sinful indulgence. She had listened with evident interest, and the Holy Spirit was, without doubt, breathing deep conviction into her soul. As the last objection to seeking Jesus *now*, trusting in him alone to do all for her, was answered, and the last prop of self-righteousness removed, this aged sinner, nearly double with years and a confirmed habit of iron strength, kneeled down with us to ask divine mercy and help. While thus engaged in prayer, 'immediately' the desire left her, and she knew in herself that she was free from that plague. The bright divine evidence of her acceptance was not received, according to her testimony, until two weeks afterwards; yet the desire for opium did not, in the interval, return; and she lived for two years a happy witness of the 'uttermost' power of Christ to save. Her unwavering testimony to the end was, 'I am no more troubled with any desire for opium than if I had never sinned in the use of it. Jesus saves me.'"

Still more astonishing is the case of a ship carpenter—Peter Banta—in Brooklyn, N. Y., also published in "Wonders of Grace," but revised by myself, from his own lips, he being under oath.

"On the 3rd of July, 1860, he received a compound fracture of the leg below the knee, by the kick of a horse and falling from a wagon.

"His physician ordered 'McMunn's Elixir of Opium,' of which, he took a whole bottle that day to relieve his terrible sufferings.

"Inflammation and ulceration supervened, and for a long period he suffered untold agony, to mitigate which he used from one to two-and-a-half bottles of the Elixir per day for nearly four years. Then, on account of the expense, he substituted morphine, consuming one drachm bottle in five days. A drachm bottle contains sixty grains; one-eighth of one grain is a full dose for an adult, consequently he used four hundred and eighty doses every five days, or ninety-six adult doses per day.

"In the course of the next five years he had increased his daily allowance to one-third of a bottle, or one hundred and sixty doses. In 1868, he heard Rev. W. H. Boole preach on the power of Grace to overcome the opium habit, and then made his first effort to break off, but in vain— the appetite was too strong. Conscience, however, was aroused, and for months he did not rest in his bed at all, but rolled upon the floor in utter wretchedness, night after night. In February, 1869, he made another attempt to break off the shackles of indulgence."

We quote at this point from " Wonders of Grace," p. 12–15 :

"And for thirty-six hours he kept to the resolution, until the reactionary effects upon his mind and body became alarming, and friends were compelled to call in the help of a number of physicians to allay his extreme excitement and prevent fatal results. These physicians, five in number, declared it necessary that he should resume the use of the morphine in order to prevent delirium or death. This he did, by taking one-half bottle, equal to two hundred and twenty doses, that night; and he continued its use for a year longer. Being satisfied there was no help in resolutions and human efforts, however well intended and sincere, he came one day to the parsonage to see me. He was in deep distress of mind, and, as he walked the floor, he exclaimed, 'What shall I do?' It was replied, 'Cease from sin; give up the use of morphine.' 'But I shall die if I do,' he replied. 'Well, die then; better so than live in sin to die at last unforgiven.' While he continued walking to and fro under deep conviction, sometimes wringing his hands, he was thus accosted: 'Why, Mr. ———, you seem to look upon yourself as some great one whose difficult case demands a mightier Saviour than the rest of mankind. You need no greater Saviour than God has provided for you and all men; and so small a thing is it for him to do to heal you, that Jesus can save a thousand just such as you, and do it with a word.

"It was a novel idea to him that Christ could save him without effort, do it at once, do it with a word; and the apprehension of this truth evidently affected him favorably, for he became calm and thoughtful.

"The following Sabbath evening, he was forward at the altar of the church, earnestly seeking the power of God for his salvation. At a suitable time it was said to him, 'There is one thing hinders you from accepting Jesus: it is your refusal to *trust him fully* to save you from the *appetite now.* On your part, say, 'Never will I again touch or taste the evil thing, though I may die; and I will trust in Jesus only to save and keep me." It was but a few minutes until he made the full surrender; and then occurred a scene which will never be forgotten by those present. The Glory of the Lord shone in his sanctuary; power from on high came upon this wretched soul whom Satan had bound, lo! these many years: his very face was illumined, while he poured forth his praises, exulting in his instantaneous and wonderful deliverance. It only remains to be added, that, from that glad hour, no desire for his former sin troubled him, no temptation to its indulgence has visited him; he is greatly improved in his physical health, and he has experienced no reaction or ill effects from the sudden disuse of the pernicious drug."

A later and enlarged edition of Mr. Boole's Tract adds the following sensible and timely remarks:

"At this date he still lives, a monument indeed of the mighty power of God. And it may be interesting to relate, as showing that the faith required to cast out 'this kind' does not necessarily produce the higher forms of intense spiritual life in the soul of the individual, that the subject of this wonderful cure, though religious, and walking in the ordinary faith of Christian life, lays no claim to a high profession, and exhibits much timidity in the exercise of faith for spiritual blessings. Many temporal difficulties have assailed him since his conversion, and these seem to affect his peace in God, filling him with doubts and fears. Nevertheless, in regard to his deliverance from the curse of opium and morphine eating, and the complete taking away of all appetite and desire for these, he is now, after five years experience, as strong and decided in his testimony as he was in the first hour.

Section 3.—The Rum Appetite.

There is as little necessity to spend time in proving the wrongfulness of this indulgence, as of the opium habit. We therefore proceed to cite the testimony in hand:

The first witness is J —— ——, who came to the Water Street Home for Women, and asked to be taken in, declaring that if she was refused, she would throw herself into the river. Her mother died when she was young, and her step-mother proved unkind.

She married a sea captain at sixteen, and by accompanying him upon his voyages, acquired the love for drink. She spoke five languages, and was worth $50,000 in her own right.

After the birth of her child, she drank worse than before, and one day left it alone—when but fifteen months' old—and went out for drink. She staid away all day and all night. Upon her return, she found her child ruptured by excessive crying, and dead. Her husband then cast her off, and she took to the street, and lived a long time in utter degradation and vice, until induced to apply at the Home.

The next day she excitedly asked permission to go out, and Mr. Bell at once saw that the demon appetite was kindling its fire afresh. He begged her to stay, and went at once to the Fulton Street Prayer Meeting, and asked prayers for her. One prayed that she might *then* have help to resist. Mr. Bell returned and found her composed and resolved. She stayed, but for three weeks could be urged no further than to ask God for Grace to keep her from yielding, meantime enduring all the gnawings of desire; but at the end of that time, she exercised faith for the immediate eradication of the appetite, and it was instantly given. She remained four months, and was then sent out to service, where she still remains, perfectly cured.

The above is given from the Records of the "Home for Women," at 273 Water Street, New York.

The following is upon the authority of Mr. Bell, Superintendent of the "Home," and Missionary in the Fourth Ward, New York, at that time:

"John D———— was born on the Isle of Wight, England, 1830.

"The son of a Presbyterian minister, he was educated for the ministry in England; and the first indication of dissipation which he gave was the formation of the habit of smoking while a student, at eighteen years of age.

"'Of course,' said he 'I must soon have its boon companion in a glass once in a while.'

"Not liquor, but beer.

"The appetite increased for four years, when it became so strong, that he felt he could not do without it, and consequently abandoned all thoughts of the ministry; but his circumstances restrained him a year longer, when he became intoxicated for the first time, and very soon after was so disgraced, that he felt obliged to leave his country and come to America.

"For two years he floated about, doing anything, and becoming more and more enslaved by his appetite. Then obtained a situation in Wall Street, where he has been ever since. His business hours closed at 2 p. m. After his morning's glass he could always control his appetite until 2 p. m., when business closed, then he would invariably become intoxicated and go home. Thus he lived for eighteen years. During all those years he was only very rarely—not oftener than once a year—in any place of worship. His wife was a backslider when he married her, but she became somewhat concerned about her soul, and attended Fulton Street Prayer Meeting, hoping to find light or relief. There she heard Mr. Fred. Bell speak of the power of God to save from any appetite, particularly strong drink; and when she got home, told her husband of what she had heard. He became interested, and asked where Bell's place was; and at last promised to go and hear him preach.

"He did so, and the text was 'Behold the man;' and from it he spoke of a salvation that would save from all sin, and particularly from strong drink. He was so interested, that neither himself or wife slept that night, but talked over the possibility of his becoming a sober, Christian man, if what he had heard was true. Next morning, the wife proposed prayer, and she tried to point him to Christ while upon their knees, but it was all dark and confused until Salvation came to *her* soul; and in ecstacies she declared to her husband that God had saved her then and there. She was a very quiet and reserved woman, and when she spoke thus positively and glowingly to him, he knew that it was so. She then pressed him to believe that Christ would save him before he arose. But he would not have Salvation unless it would deliver him from his twin appetites for rum and tobacco. He did not know as he could have it, but he resolved to believe for it, and then trust God to keep him. On going to his business he had to pass the liquor shops where he had been accustomed to procure his morning glass, and found no desire whatever for his dram.

"'So far,' said he, 'all right!'

"Then, too, he found he had no desire for his morning smoke. All day in business everything went so smoothly that it 'seemed like Sunday.' He went home sober that night at an early hour for the first time in many years. He went to the 'Home' and testified to all this, and no reaction took place either from the tobacco habit of twenty-five years or the liquor habit of twenty years, but he felt buoyant as in his youth.

"About eleven months have now elapsed, and his old appetites have never revived."

Here follows a case narrated by an associate, the subject himself having gone where no temptations come:

"There lived among us a backslider, a respected man; some losses he met with caused him to take to the bottle, and for something like twenty years he seldom drew a sober breath. He was filthy in his conversation so that he was shunned except by his boon companions; but he had a praying wife, and for twenty years she followed him night and day with her prayers. God heard and answered in a wonderful manner. He laid him upon what all thought was his death bed, but in His loving mercy He pardoned his heart-wanderings and blest him with Salvation, and a more lovely Christian it would be hard to find. I worked with him a good deal after his restoration, and never enjoyed working with any one as I did with brother R———. The ungodly were constrained to say, 'What a change in old Eph!' as they used to call him. He assured me often that he had not the least appetite for rum. He thought that he could stand up to his knees in it, and have no desire for it; and he could scarcely praise God enough for his deliverance. Thus he lived for about two years a faithful Christian; then he took a bad cold which settled on his lungs, and he never rallied. But his chamber was a Bethel; it was good to be there, quite on the verge of Heaven. So patient, so resigned and happy, he passed away, and his last words were, 'For me to live is Christ; but to die is gain.'"

The good old lady whose testimony appears upon page 72, writes concerning her brother-in-law, and husband—both drunkards at one time—that both were cured by prayer, the former instantaneously, who lived eighteen years without the least desire for it, while her husband, cured a little more gradually, has been living now twenty-six years fully saved from all craving for liquor.

The experience of Fred. Bell is so remarkable, that we give it as taken from his own lips expressly for this work.

He had been drinking ten years, but had been an habitual drunkard seven years; was converted when under the influence of liquor.

The reaction caused by suddenly giving up the use of liquor brought on *delirium tremens*, and for three weeks he "passed through all the horrors of hell." Then told his wife that he could bear it no longer; and unless the religion, which the missionary by whose labors he had been converted had told him of, could save him from this appetite, he must die or drink. So he went to the missionary and told him the same. He suggested signing the pledge. After it was done, Bell said: "Sir, won't you pray to God for me, that I may be able to keep this pledge?"

Putting his hand on Bell's shoulder,

the missionary replied: "My boy, I want you to pray with me, that God will take away the appetite!"

This aroused his curiosity, and he went home and told his wife what Mr. Gregg had said, and added, "It seems too much; but it will be for His glory, and I think He will do it."

So both agreed to pray for it; and after praying half an hour, during which time his wife repeatedly asked him, "Is it gone yet?" at length he exclaimed, "Lord, take it away or I die!" when a strange feeling passed over him, and he arose and said: "Wife, I feel a funny happy; so glad; but it's funny glad!" "But is it gone?" said she. "I don't know, but I'm so funny glad!" Five years subsequent experience has proved that the appetite was entirely eradicated just then. And three years later the appetite for tobacco, which had been indulged to excess for fifteen years, was instantly removed in answer to prayer.

Again we quote from Mr. Boole's Tract, adding our conviction that Christians might do great good by distributing it freely among those who need its encouragement:

"It was about seven years ago when, on an afternoon, there came to our residence a man whom we had known for several years. He was of excellent family, had an estimable Christian wife, and his children, now grown to manhood, were intelligent and respectable. But this father was a drunkard. For many years he had been addicted to the cup, and all efforts of friends had failed to produce any lasting effect upon him. Mortification and shame had stricken his family, and, as is usual, not himself alone was the sufferer by his vice, but the innocent were dragged down with him. As he entered the room, on the occasion above referred to, a glance at his face showed signs of deep feeling and dejection of spirit. 'What shall I do, sir; my wife is almost heart-broken; I am a disgrace to my children, and I cannot break away from this dreadful habit of drinking.' These were among his first utterances.

"'Have you tried to break off from drinking?'

"'Tried,' said he, 'tried! I have walked these streets 'till two o'clock in the morning, many a time, in the agony of my soul, because of my wretched condition. I have resolved against drink a hundred times, yet I cannot pass a liquor saloon, but I *must* go in and get a drink. What *shall* I do?' 'Have you prayed for help from God?' 'Yes; I have resolved and prayed, but it is no use; when the appetite comes on I can't resist.' 'What have you prayed for?' 'Why, that God would give me power to overcome the appetite and temptation to drink.' 'Ah, that has been your mistake to pray to *overcome* the appetite. Have you not thought that God is able to *extinguish* the fiery appetite and thirst for liquor?' This was our reply to the enslaved drunkard. It was a new idea to the man, and he looked as if he would have said, 'Tell me that again.' We continued: 'You ought to be able to pass every rum-shop and liquor saloon as safely and unconcernedly as we do. This thirst for strong drink is unnatural and sinful. Now, God is able to save to the *uttermost;* and surely your sad case is included in the margin of 'uttermost.' Your resolutions to do better are of no value, because this sinful habit has broken your will-power, and your resolution is born of a weak and enfeebled nature; too weak indeed to contend against your fearfully strong appetite. It is not the will of your Heavenly Father that you should longer go fettered and bound in the chains of this slavery. Nor does He desire you should pray to overcome what He is ready and able at once to *destroy*—this craving for a sinful thing. But you must trust in the Lord Jesus Christ, and His power to save you *now*,—save you most fully and keep you saved. Now, the Holy Spirit will do all this *in* you: He is '*the power that worketh in us;*' and the word of promise is, 'He is more willing to *give* the Holy Spirit to them that ask than we are to give good gifts unto our children.' Will you accept of His help and yield yourself up to His power?' This anxious man seemed to comprehend the situation at a glance: he was in a condition to grasp at any real and substantial support; and as he seriously answered, 'I will; I do,' we knelt to pray. The prayer was very short; for the dear Lord needs no urging when real *need* and *faith* agree to accept His grace. When he rose we said, 'Now, don't avoid the corner shops if your duties call you to walk the streets; you are to walk in liberty, and are *more than* conqueror through Him who is able to keep you from falling. Let Him do it for you; abandon yourself to Him, and wherever we can safely go, you can also go.' This man left the house a saved being in soul and body. He united with the Church, and lived a consistent life. ' But did the cure last ? Was there no return of the desire, the thirst?'

"Well, four years after this interview, he having in the mean time removed from the neighborhood, we met him as he walked in one of the avenues. We found that he was engaged in a lawful business, but which required him, however, to associate with drinking men, and spend part of his time in the neighborhood of liquor saloons. 'How about your old taste, and habit of drinking?' we asked. He smiled and looked happy, as he earnestly replied, 'Oh, I have never from that day tasted a drop, have not had the slightest desire for any, nor temptation to it;' and his face, with both his eyes, verified the statement."

SEC. 4.—THE HABIT OF IRRITABILITY.

We first give place to a letter from an intelligent physician in a southern city.

August 16, 1873.

Dear Sir:

"Observing your queries in to-day's *Home Journal,* I am moved to write you.

"I cannot yet claim entire sanctification, but I feel that I am advancing, and gaining knowledge of the way by experience.

"I find in myself that irritability of nerves from duty required despite exhaustion, &c, extends or not, to the moral sphere proper, (abating benevolence and stirring up temper,) exactly in accord with my *willingness to endure* the physical distress for the Lord's sake. If I am, it does not ruffle the temper, only gives me a 'gone feeling' about the head or heart, or drowsiness, or something else, physically, with the distinct thought of God caring, and graduating the burden wisely and well, perhaps on purpose to devitalize this body, and so to shorten my pilgrim way; perhaps only to kill out all trust in physical power to supplement grace in the carrying on of the inward work of holiness. A good meal, an ice cream, a nap of sleep, or an excursion, or company, may be indicated as according to His will, for amelioration; but if the way be barred, it is a distinct call to suffer *with Christ*, in which, you know, is much cause to rejoice, even though the occasion be little. If not barred, then it may be taken, assuring myself that it is done also as unto Him.

"On the contrary, if my will refuses the burden and cross, of perpetual demand for brick without the complement of straw wherewith to make it; if I resent the order of Providence, which places me in such a position, I will as surely so far hate, or cease to love persons who are the instrument or occasion of it, and even look upon the Lord Himself as an Israelite would upon his taskmaster, or as a prisoner would on an arbitrary or at least thoughtless jailor. Temper then displays itself.

"*Such felt irritability* is clearly incompatible with a holy heart, being an imputation against the wisdom, benevolence, and care of the Master, and a variance of my will from His, who calls me to endure, but I object. All is due to *defective consecration.*"

Mothers and housekeepers will appreciate the force of the following, which speaks for itself:

"I want to say to the glory of God that I have been kept from all sense of irritability, while in a state of nervous exhaustion, under circumstances that were very trying, with the cares of a family pressing upon me, and with very poor help."

Now comes one, fifty-nine years a conqueror. A man of God of hoary head and saintly heart, who needs no voucher to those who know him as one of the veteran itinerants of the past:

"You desire *matters of fact* in experiences. To save copying your questions, I will refer to them by their numbers.

1. My natural temperament is nervous, irritable; yet, after I was sanctified, October 26th, 1809, I did not for *three* years feel my passions ruffled or disturbed; though often placed in the most trying circumstances, and the greatest of provocations, such as, if I had not been under the power of saving grace, would have caused anger and retaliation. Feeling called of God to preach, but being repulsed by the preachers because I was so young (eighteen); before I was aware of it, my mind became despondent, and I became irritable, and remained so for two years, though I never lost the evidence of justification. If the irritability rose so as to feel the least degree of anger, I had to repent, pray, and obtain forgiveness, before I could feel peace in my soul. After two years in this state, I regained the evidence of perfect love, and now for fifty-nine years have been without a cloud in that particular; and I often wonder at the mercy and grace of God that have

kept me in this state, and *feel* that it is of grace, and not of myself.

"Do not understand me as being free from temptation when 'in a state of nervous exhaustion,' or at other times, but I am not conscious of any stronger temptations when in that state, than when not; my strongest temptations have been when under nervous excitement, not exhaustion. I have often felt a sense of the wrong done me, and felt grieved on account of it, but felt no anger, hatred, ill-will, or like retaliating.

"It has been, and is, a question in my mind, what standard of holiness, or Christian perfection, we have in the Bible? or what allowance God makes for human infirmities? Job was 'a perfect man,' at least God said so; but he said things that I could not, and feel a clear conscience. I could not curse the day of my birth, nor wish I had not been born. I have not the least idea that I am *more* than perfect, or more so than Job was, yet I could not do as he did.

"It is said in Scripture that 'God is *angry* with the wicked every day,' and of Christ it is said, 'he looked upon them with *anger*, being grieved at their unbelief.' In what this anger consists, is the question. I cannot for a moment think it is like *human* anger; or contains in it a revengeful feeling. God is said to have been 'grieved to the heart,' at the wicked ways of the Israelites; and Christ was grieved at the unbelief of those who witnessed his miracles, but did not believe in his Messiahship. But judging from my own feeling, I cannot think of the Divine anger meaning anything more than a high sense of disapproval; and yet abundant in mercy, and willing to forgive.

"2. The *felt* irritability, whatever it may arise from, may be only the temptation, and no sin, if not yielded to; and as Christ was tempted, yet without sin, so we may be tempted, and yet be 'consistent with a holy heart,' if we don't yield to it. Bodily infirmities may be the *occasion* of the temptation, as 'hunger, was of Christ; and the temptation may have more power in it from this circumstance; but God's grace is sufficient.

'He will not suffer us to be tempted *above* what we are able.' This has been *my* experience."

We have looked in vain over the following letters for some portion to omit, but the lucid statements of facts, all so interesting, ought to be read as they are written; and therefore are inserted entire.

The second letter was in answer to personal inquiries, addressed to the writer by the author of this treatise:

Sept. 15, 1873.

My dear Brother in Christ:

"As I opened the *Advocate* for September, my eye fell first on your 'card,' and with eager interest I perused the very important questions given therewith. It is not without much prayerfulness, and some very intimate communings with God as to His will in the matter, that I have concluded to reply to the first of these. The query is very carefully and concisely put; and to it, just as it stands, accepting its phraseology just as it would naturally be understood, I will say to the glory of God, yes. I have proven that one 'of a nervous temperament' *can* 'be so kept by the power of grace that in a time of continual strain of duties, and *while in* a state of nervous exhaustion' she 'shall be free from all sense of irritability. 'I would add to this an emphasis by saying, that after fifteen years of invalidism, as a great sufferer, and my whole nervous system become a wreck, I was in that condition mentioned, where 'irritability' had become to me almost a second nature. I confess, too, that prior to all this I was as a child, very quick tempered; yet I find God's 'grace' *is* sufficient to keep us, even in extreme cases, from falling. To Jesus be everlasting honors paid!

"In reviewing the 'card,' I see that you ask not only a reply, but 'a statement *of such experience.* Mine is one so very personal that I have never written it, and but to one friend has it been told.

"However I give it, that you understanding the case may cull such items as you choose. It was found necessary in the Fall of 1869 that I should undergo a series of medical treatment which called me daily to New York (*did* for nine months); I had scarce strength to get there and return, spending all the interval in my bed. Soon after this commenced, it was decided that I must submit almost to starvation, in order to reduce my flesh, and this extreme abstinence was to continue three months. I should say that my cure—all for nervous pains—had long been in the use of tea and extra food. These both taken from me, I was almost beside myself, and every symptom connected with the disordered state of my general nervous system was aggravated. Naught but great will power on my part, and my confidence in the will and judgment of my Dr. took me through. Then I had not learned to say 'Thou art my strength.'

"About that time I was taken, an entire novice, to the Tuesday meeting, (Dr. Palmer's). It made me weaker and sicker every time; so that I scarcely made up my physical loss during the week; and yet so *terrible* was my spiritual condition, that wise friends, dear souls deeply taught of the Spirit bade me go. If words could avail I would *praise*

Jesus now for that, inasmuch as it was the means blessed to the *healing* of my soul, *after* this the body recovered from untold chronic suffering of fifteen years standing.

"We pass now to a time, when that extreme fasting had ceased, and the abstemious diet I used was by contrast quite a luxury for me. I had come in the meanwhile to be well enough to be *very busy*; and moreover I had learned to trust Jesus for and with *every thing*. There was no department in my life into which this trust did not enter. As I became more active, I ventured to eat more but soon found that my weight increased. I knew into what condition my head was put by former fasting, and the question came up 'Ought I to try it, and thereby perhaps be disabled to perform this work the Lord gives me to do for Him?' I went to God with it, and in a way to which I was then unaccustomed, that prayer took the form of dialogue. As though we walked arm in arm. He talked with me. I asked if indeed it were worth while, and if I should venture. He replied, 'Canst thou *trust me?*' I said, 'yes, Lord—but in what direction shall I turn?' He asked, *if I would go as* He told me. I promised to, if so be I might only *see Him* leading, so as to know the way. Then he fastened upon me the query, ' *Whithersoever*?' At this point I felt still willing, but oh, so pressed! If he had walked me up to the very edge of a precipice, and said step forward—it would not have tried me more. (By faith I took that step.) As we reached this point I cried out, '*Yes*, Lord, only let thine everlasting arm be *underneath* me.'

"From that time I felt directed to pursue again those extreme means, and had the assurance too, that I should not be unable to work on, in the use of ordinary mental power, even while the natural *supply* was cut off!

"I tried it, and it was even so. Nay more, my writing and study increased upon me, but no physical inability stood in the way.

"I considered it an unusual and precious triumph; due all of it to ' *the power of grace.*'

"I may add, that so habituated to God's

keeping power am I, that though *frequently* 'in a state of nervous *exhaustion*' quite severe, the irritability does *not come*.

"At the time referred to above, I found in my dreams still the old tendency to 'temper.' I could not think it 'consistent with a holy heart,' or even possible in one *fully saved*. I felt as responsible and condemned as though it were the sin of my waking hours. I looked to Jesus *for*, and by a specific faith *claimed*, victory just there. I need only say He kept His promise, and according to my faith it was to me. I cannot think that a 'disordered bodily condition' justifies us in aught which under the same 'conditions' we should not find in Christ Jesus."

Sept. 20th, 1873.

Rev. S. H. P.:

Dear Sir:—Yours is received, and in view of its request I am finding myself in rather an odd position. Inasmuch as I am wholly the Lord's; all that I have is His, for whatever purpose it will subserve. And yet, to give to a stranger, and to others indefinitely these confidences so personal, is altogether contrary to my natural tastes. My life is aptly described in one of Dr. Holland's lines, as made of 'unwritten histories, unfathomed mysteries.' I cannot, however, decline so to do, for the hope I have that some weak, tempted soul may find herein a bit of comfort, or ray of hope or light. Oh, that all such would *see* the enormous sin of limiting God's power!

"In September, 1851, I had a violent attack of typhoid fever, which ran without a break forty-two days, and I all that time in a delirium. One after another three attending physicians gave up the case; and only a mother's care outran the disease. It was induced by severe mental tax at school, followed by a great grief, and some very trying dentistry which called me daily to take a long, hot walk. My nervous system was shattered, and my poor head almost useless; so for years it continued, and I a victim of neuralgia coming daily to any part of my body. After that, I settled down into a nervous headache, which was *seldom* a day gone; and worse than this, *dyspepsia*. I know it in all its forms, and can fully appreciate the numberless 'side issues' that come of it. While away at school, I had fallen from a high swing on a stony place; and during these years of weakness my back refused longer to ignore it—it ached a great deal.

"Previous to any of this (and up to my cure in 1869), I had been really afflicted with *acute* periodic suffering, and grown very nervous and *morbid*, just from the dread of pains, so intolerable. My late increase of flesh tended, the doctor thought, to apoplexy; hence his haste in depleting me. My diet was for three months *only* a small piece of lean meat twice a day, and a little sour fruit, just enough food to prevent disease from ruining my stomach. No drinks allowed except cold water, and that only between meals. So you see, the 'complications' were enough! Medicine of all the schools, and water treatment, had been given me without benefit.

"Naturally of a sanguine temperament, I thought each time I should be cured, and in each failure was almost killed with disappointment. I had resolved that henceforth no power of persuasion should ever tempt me to try any remedy, nor would I ever again *hope* for relief.

"With the thought, however, that my spared life was for some purpose, and that as I was 'twas worse than useless—that I was a cumberer of the ground—I didn't *dare* keep that vow. I was overpersuaded, and did undertake Swedish movements. I was not only cured in all respects, but have *remained so*.

"Now a word about my good, *kind* doctor; and it's for God's glory, not in the spirit of criticism. He is a man of quick sympathies, strong will and great magnetic power. My friend who had been his patient, advised me to yield myself to his influence; and when I was so weak through depletion, I found that it was my only comfort; I felt as if I were carried, while resting on his will and hopefulness. He however was an infidel, and far more gifted in argument than I. I was seeking health, *and Jesus;* he to cure me by equalizing forces —that is, to tax and develop my muscular system, and *quiet* the mental. He forbade all brain work. I obeyed scrupulously, except Tuesdays. His patients were like him, and yet though I was with them at his room, that hot bed of infidelity, two hours daily, Jesus *held* me. I was learning the way of full salvation, despite a weak body, and the firmest educational prejudices that ever a blue Pres' had to combat. The meeting sickened me, because I was kicking *hard* against the pricks, and for six months I went through a constant crucifixion. I disliked the peculiarities of the place, but yet could not stay away, and being so fascinated, continued to go, till 'by the power of grace' I yielded to the Spirit's call.

"If your patience is not already exhausted, permit a few words not just to the point. In my consecration I found so little to give to Jesus—only my *will* and my pen. He had chosen to use the latter. With it He keeps me busy wooing and winning souls to entire sanctification. I, who had been a church member eighteen years, and *full* of unbelief (but didn't know it), can now, in utmost tenderness and patience, bear with others. I find the church is full of unbelief! I ask your prayers for God's blessing on my work. It's all His, and I but the tool used. You see now why I was so led to reply to those very ' questions,' the which are so often glossed over by the Tempter. Sick ones verily think they may run on with a loose rein. Oh, that *God's will* were paramount with all who name the name of Christ!"

We have thus cited unimpeachable testimony upon the several habits of tobacco, strong drink, opium, and irritability, and leave the *facts* with the reader, abstaining from comment, only asking him to read again pp. 9–11, and then judge impartially, as the evidence demands, and *act* as the Holy Spirit may suggest.

SEC. 5.—THE HABIT OF LUST.

Mr. Bell thus narrates the case of a

Mr. —— ——, a Custom House officer, 33 years of age, stout and full of animal spirits, who spent his entire salary of between $3,000 and $4,000, and all his spare time on fast horses and loose women. He was not an excessive drinker. By some means he was induced to visit the meetings at the Water Street "Home," and was there converted. The first week after, he was exceedingly troubled with lascivious desire, and strongly tempted to resort again to the houses of ill-fame. Just then, he heard about "FULL SALVATION," and concluded that he did not want a religion that could not save him "*fully*" in that particular direction. He sought at once, and found the peace of perfect trust. The result has been, he has been kept through severe trials, and still stands, the only Christian among three hundred fellow laborers, and is one of the brightest lights of the —— —— Church.

The Western minister whose testimony upon the tobacco habit has already been cited on page 66 further writes:

" As to question 5, if it refers to *appe-*

tites simply, and not to passions, then it applies to myself. As to passions, this was not my besetment, though it was the Doctor's just mentioned. But in respect to my appetite and his passions, in no instance that we can recollect has the peace of the soul been disturbed—only ruffled on the surface—for we had 'come to him and found rest to our souls.' I believe we are kept from its desire even, by a power above nature. The capacity for its use was never destroyed, but He sanctified it, purified it, and, subject to the conditions of all salvation, He has silenced its demands. Here are the experiences of two in these different ages of life, viz : the Doctor is upwards of fifty, while I am only twenty-five."

The physician whose letter appears upon page 107, relative to irritability, says:

"On your last two questions I can also speak from experience, not as to momentary, but rather gradual release; yet remaining but partial—but I trust advancing with increasing speed to the moment of entire deliverance. The gradual part is, I know, simply due to a gradual consecration of details, as dependent on a gradual increase of light upon those details, with equal increase of conviction, on which the general matter largely hinges with me. (I do not refer to drinking, or anything of that sort, but to an appetite of equal power, the gratification of which is providentially circumscribed to a degree that has been an infinite source of disquiet and temptation). But certainly Jesus was tempted in this also, and can keep my body pure, and mind also, by the power which kept His own.

"But I find the *same answer to this query as to the first.* The whole matter turns on the questions, does God order it? does God care? Am I willing to forego my 'natural rights' in this respect, and to *endure* the spoliation for His sake? Or, again, do I, doubting His care, resent, refuse, and take the bit between my teeth, mentally; chafing under the infliction? If so, at every solicitation, conflict; if not, peace! I alternate these experiences as yet. God grant full consecrating power to finally settle all.

I remain, fraternally yours,

————.''

A very sincere brother writes:

"My experience is, that these stronger appetites of the organism are all subdued in perfect consecration to the will of Jesus, to possess us, and use the grace given. A full consecration of our powers and members to Jesus is sufficient to make us proof against any temptation, to a known evil, that will mar the peace of the soul."

The following contains sound argument as well as good experience:

"If I understand question fifth, I answer, Yes. This is a *natural* and God-given appetite, and one of the things for which we ought to *thank* God as much as for a natural appetite for food. Connubial pleasure is one of the things which should make us love God more, and which does make us love him more when our heart is right. If we yield to imagination, we shall, in all probability, find discord. Though Paul had a thorn in the flesh, yet the grace of God was sufficient for him, and he could glory.

"The Devil tempts men through the imagination in a very large degree, painting seeming prospective pictures of pleasure and bliss; there is where the discord gets in. If a man would fortify himself with truth, filling his mind with it to repletion, he would have no room for imagination.

"There is nothing in nature or natural appetites, any of them, that need to disturb, or that will disturb, the peace of God. They enhance that peace. God does not work against himself. Jesus says, 'For this reason God made them male and female.'

"God has power over hereditary desire, or perverted, as much as over anything.

"Something of this I know, for amativeness was so strong in me, as to produce a positive deformity of my head, being the largest organ on my head by considerable, and showed itself before I could walk readily; yet God has kept me, that I have never slipped. Jesus came to save men from sin, not from temptation, further than as Paul says, 'that ye may be able to bear it.' Christ makes the way to escape from sin now as much as ever."

As this work is designed for general circulation, it might be deemed indelicate to insert the very detailed and explicit testimonies which have been received upon this point.

The author has therefore prepared a *Private Treatise* for both sexes, called *Princely Manhood*, discussing the subject as briefly as is consistent with a fair presentation of facts, means and methods of self-control and soul-victory, and detailing testimony at length of a most astounding character from persons of unquestionable veracity.

In order that the *subject* may be *justly* represented in these pages, and no opportunity of good to the reader be allowed to pass unimproved, we transcribe some of the many evidences that we are from time to time receiving, of its great utility and almost unequaled helpfulness, drawn mainly from private sources, because the book has not been furnished for editoria criticism, save in a few instances. The delicacy of the subject, and the great necessity for information of the right kind, are our apologies for the insertion of the following pages, and from the evidence contained in the book to which these pages refer, it is proved unquestionably that even those of a strong amative tendency, and habituated to frequent indulgence, may become in a very short time so reconstructed in this department of their nature, that TOTAL ABSTINENCE shall be pleasure so PEACEFULLY maintained, that they will wonder at the vehemence of their former passions.

BOSTON, Mass., June, 1874.

Dear Brother Platt:
"I like your your 'Princely Manhood' much. I pray God to bless it to the good of many.

Yours, in Jesus,
CHARLES CULLIS."

Mass., May 23, 1874.

My Dear Sir:—I have examined with interest your little work on "Princely Manhood." It is clear, earnest, and pure.

I trust it meets a large sale. Its entire freedom from mercenary and other unworthy motives, gives it a strong claim upon the attention of parents. I do not see why you should say, "for adults only." I should be more than willing to have a daughter or son of ten or twelve years of age read and study every line of it. Hoping that you will use every honorable means to secure a broad distribution of this admirable little work, I am,

Yours very truly,

Dio Lewis.

The following is from a widely known clergyman in the West:

Your valuable publication entitle "Princely Manhood," fell into my hands a few days ago. I must say that I was astonished when I read it. I am pretty well posted on the subjects treated therein; have read a great deal on those and kindred subjects, but this little book handled the matter so unlike other authors, and pointed out the *right way* so plainly, and altogether, wrote from a stand-point so different, that I was greatly delighted in its perusal. I shall feel it my duty as a

Christian minister, to circulate "Princely Manhood." I have been thinking very lately, "Where can I find a work of this kind that I can recommend—one that is not tinctured with infidelity in some of its forms?" From my acquaintance with Rev. S. H. Platt as an author, and from what I have seen of this book, I think it will do a vast amount of good where circulated.

A business man of culture and varied experience writes thus from a New England city:

The main purpose of this writing is to thank you for "Princely Manhood," a copy of which I saw yesterday for the first time. I have read it through twice. I am forty-six years old, have read many books and more men, but in this little book now for the first time have seen a plain statement of a truth I have known to exist. This generation will die unsaved, but the time will come when good men will understand and obey this truth that you have so modestly set forth. *I know how much need there is of it, and could write a volume of illustrative facts to prove its neces-*

sity. Yet how few see it! I have talked with good men, who admitted the beauty of the theory, but denied that it is practical; but I KNOW it to be so!

Another, in high official position, in Brooklyn, N. Y., writes:

Acquaintance with its truths will be of inestimable value to all who seek high moral or Christian attainments. It is a scientific, philosophical and christianly showing of matters most intimately connected with human welfare, and of which most persons are deplorably ignorant.

From Brooklyn also comes the following endorsement by one of its most successful physicians:

The theme is one that has been thought to belong only to my own profession, yet I see no objection to its careful handling by any prudent minister who is sufficiently acquainted with the related sciences to speak intelligently about it. Your own treatment of the subject is thoroughly scientific, intensely practical, chaste in expression, and, in its exhibition of the helpfulness of Grace, greatly exalting to one's conception of the Gospel as a Cure for human sin. It will not *only* do *good*, but just the *kind* of good most *needed*.

Another intelligent and successful physician writes from a city in Connecticut:

Its influence for good upon the lives and health of those who read it can scarcely be estimated. I believe it will harmonize many domestic difficulties, and so instruct parents that children will be saved from many pernicious habits.

A clergyman, of Boston, says: "It ought to be read by every adult in the world."

Another, in Brooklyn, affirms: "The subject is treated in a very chaste and refined manner, evincing great research, and I earnestly recommend it."

Another writes: "It is a mighty incentive to true, royal, christian manhood."

While still another writes thus: "After untold suffering, induced by vicious habits before my conversion, and years of almost hopeless struggle, I have been wonderfully saved in a very short time by the method advocated in 'Princely Manhood.'"

The following we give unabridged from the man who is better qualified, perhaps, than any other in the Brooklyn pulpit, to speak intelligently and discriminatingly on this subject:

BROOKLYN, May 8, 1874.

Dear Bro. Platt :—I have at length read your "Princely Manhood" with great care. I could not conscientiously give my criticism till I had thoroughly examined it. And now I shall speak, not as a reviewer, but as a brother who enters into the spirit of the book with ardent feeling as well as careful thought. Other books of great value have been written upon this subject, and many more will be, and, on account of the immense importance thereof, need be. Some of these I have read, and none without seeing in them excellencies. Your work, however, *excels them all in this, that it looks at the subject from the stand-point of exalted spiritual life.* It considers sexual functions as pertaining to the most elevated character, notes their abuses as crimes against the highest laws of our being, locates the real seat of abuse in the mind and heart, and presents conclusively the all-sufficient power of the saving Grace of God as a remedy of universal application. It opens with an ennobling view of the Sexual Powers, allowing to them a high and commanding place. It glorifies them with purity, showing their ministry to the growth of the affections.

Chapter IV. presents a startling array of citations, proving the prevalence of the abuse by which this book was made necessary. As a warning, I think the chapter will do great good, especially because other chapters in connection with it offer such certain help.

The addresses to the Married and to Parents, showing the far-reaching effects and unmeasured evils attendant upon marital excess, should be before the eyes of the heads of every household.

When you so strongly present the blessings of "*the sanctified disuse* of any faculty or function which Providence bars out of legitimate opportunity," you lay open one of the noblest manifestations of a true faith in God and obedience to Him. A volume might be evolved from the broad truth here opened.

Chapter VIII., on the Attainment of Harmony between sexual life and the highest spiritual aspirations, expresses, all too briefly, yet to the thoughtful mind with distinguishing clearness, the practical relation which the higher reason should assume toward the physical man. I cannot tell you how earnestly I endorse the several rules here laid down, viz., the entire Reconciliation to Sex, which ends the struggle of the man with himself; the declaration that normal sexual excitement is a sacred activity; that it cannot, in the heaven-ordained course of nature, be avoided, and that the power of the Grace of God is sufficient to reconcile, sanctify, and control this faculty of human life.

Your conclusions are most wise and acceptable, and the state of Glorious Rest to which the following of your practical directions inevitably leads, is as certain as it is desirable. When parents take your advice, men will be numerously saved and God greatly glorified.

In conclusion, my dear Brother Platt, I must say, its statements are so clear, its conclusions so sound, its spirit so pure and exalted that I would fully recommend it to all the world.

It has no doubt appeared to you, as it clearly does to me, that the work could be greatly expanded, and that thus enlarged, many of its positions might be more extensively enforced, so as to make it more impressive to common minds. It bears throughout the mark of a condensation almost too severe. Yet your object being to make a popular book which should be recommended to large circulation by its small expense, makes this excusable.

Great is the work to be done in this department of instruction. Take comfort in the fact that a part of that work you have well done, lifting the subject to the only plane where Christ, by the Holy

Ghost, saves and sanctifies the whole man.

I remain, with full sympathy and sincere love,
>Yours in Christ,

The *Methodist Home Journal*, April 4th, 1874, says:

Rev. S. H. Platt, A. M., author of several publications of an intensely spiritual character, has lately issued a treatise entitled "Princely Manhood," in which the sexual relations are viewed from a religious stand-point. It is well said that purity of thought is the most difficult attainment in the Christian life, and the author, in his attempt to elevate the struggling aspirant to a life of rectitude has evinced a brave indifference to prurient sensibilities, and a noble aim to benefit humanity. We could wish that this outspoken, honest, and convincing book might go forth, not only to correct existing evils, but prevent the demoralization caused by such infamous literature as tends only to inflame passion and ruin body and soul. The salvation of the Gospel, it is maintained, is for both, and to all the helpless there is afforded hope, and certainty of victory by faith in the Lord Jesus Christ.

The *World's Crisis*, Boston, March 25th, says:

"Princely Manhood" is the title of a new book of much value, just issued by Rev. S. H. Platt, Bridgeport, Ct. The fact that it comes from his pen affords a surety that it is worth reading. This is "a private treatise, for adults only," treating upon "the procreative instinct, as related to moral and christian life." *It is truly a book for the times, and of great value to all for whom it is designed.*

We fully endorse the following statements in relation to the work:

"This work is one of rare interest and value, and 'should be read,' says a Boston editor, 'by every man in the world.' It treats the subject of the author's lecture on the same name more in detail, and is a mine of rich suggestion to the middle aged and young. Except the Bible, no father can give his child a more valuable literary keepsake than this. Millions of money and years of health would be saved if men would heed its words."

We recommend the book to all for whom it was prepared, as one of special value, particularly to those who are anxious to enjoy pure religion.

Says Mrs. Anna Wittenmyer of Philadelphia, in the *Christian Woman*, April, 1874:

"Princely Manhood" is the name of a modest little book that has found its way to our table.

The author, Rev. S. H. Platt, is a clear, able thinker, and a writer of some reputation, and although he handles a delicate subject, his language is so well chosen and modest that we find nothing objectionable, as far as we have examined the book. We are sorry that we have not had time to give it a careful reading.

We have long felt that if parents knew more of the physiological laws of their own being, and the appetites and temptations that their children have to contend with, they would train them more intelligently, and thousands who fall annually the victims of sinful appetites and passion, would be saved. *We advise parents to read this book.*

The following appeared (not as an advertisement) in *The Daily Standard*, of Bridgeport, Ct., April, 1874:

We recall attention to the book lately published by Rev. S. H. Platt, in order to publish some extracts from a letter written by a gentleman connected with the Associated Press of New York, which speaks for itself. Our only qualification is that it is adapted to both sexes, and should be read by both.

Dear Mr. Platt:—In acknowledging the receipt of your unequaled lecture on "Princely Manhood," let me thank you for the soul feast I had in reading it. You have given, in my judgment, the only *practical* solution of this much vexed question. Could I have but read this work years ago it would have shed much light on a dark pathway. I never supposed that *from temptation you would evolve strength to resist temptation.* This you have substantially done. The more I think of it the stranger it seems to me that ministers of the gospel should so long have held their peace. This I can only regard as reprehensible in the extreme. *Where the most light is needed, there we find utter darkness.* The subject is mainly handled *from mercenery* motives by quacks and charlatans, who, with their illustrated works, but pour gunpowder into a magazine already on fire.

I shall take great pains to circulate this lecture and have already called attention to it through the press. Were I able I would place it in the hands of every young man able to receive the truth, and bid him find therein the firm yet gentle guidance his wavering soul is longing for.

If your lecture to ladies* is half as ably gotten up, I think you owe it to a suffering generation to place it in their hands as speedily as possible.

---

* Referring to a work in preparation, called "QUEENLY WOMANHOOD," for females only.

CHAPTER III.

The Power of Grace in extirpating special Inborn Perversities.

This subject is given the prominence of a distinct chapter, not because its importance merits it, but in order more forcibly to meet the excuse which so many are ready to urge, viz.: "My habit is natural, I was born with it; have had a craving for indulgence all my life," etc., as if this fact presented any insurmountable barrier to reform. Undoubtedly, it is more difficult for one unaided by prayer to overcome, where the perversity is an evil heritage of the birth. But, in providing for human wants, God was not forgetful of these inborn aptitudes and tendencies, which are counted among "all your needs," that God will supply—see Phil. 4:19.

The careful reader may note, in many of the instances already detailed, e. g. pp. 72–78, that the appetite or habit had existed from childhood, and yet deliverance was found. We have never yet heard of a case of complete and constant trust in Christ for help, without the requisite aid being realized; and we hold it to be not only theologically but philosophically impossible that it should be otherwise. Let it be settled, then, once for all, that the prayer of faith attended by suitable effort, will in EVERY case extirpate inborn perversities, as such, and give peace to the soul.

CHAPTER IV.

The Power of Grace in giving soul-rest in control of the Natural Appetites.

Unlike perversities, the natural appetites are not to be expunged. They are good in their sphere, and their legitimate indulgence need never form a hindrance to spiritual development. But they must be under the control of Christian motives.

As servants they are not to be despised, but as masters they become perversities which must be destroyed.

The appetite for food, and the sexual impulse, are all that need to be named in this connection; and the last only to refer the reader again to *"Princely Manhood"* for full information.

As civilization progresses in any race, the arts, which are originated by and constitute a part of the development, create a troop of artificial wants, often more pressing as they are more numerous than our natural wants.

Among these, the culinary art has ever held a high place; and luxurious living has been its concomitant. The gustatory appetite, pampered by trained indulgence from the very cradle, becomes almost insatiable, until people seem to "live to eat," rather than "eat to live." The consequence is diseases of divers forms, producing more or less mental depression and nervous irritability, both acting unfavorably upon the religious character.

The Sacred Book classes gluttons with wine bibbers, undoubtedly upon the principle that "diseased or depressed conditions of the body do, in a large measure, affect and determine our quality of thoughts, and our quality of thoughts determines our quality of purpose in life." Says Dr. J. C. Jackson, (Gluttony Plague, p. 24.)

"It is not surprising to me that Christians are so cold, formal, and unimpulsive as they are. It is obvious why they should be so. They are so gross in bodily appetite, and so indulgent in the sphere of the passions, that the descent of the Holy Spirit is impossible under its ORDINARY plan of approach to the human soul. A vast majority of Christians, simply because of bad habits in physical life, go for years with no GLOWING light from the Divine finding its way into their souls. They live in the shadow of that light altogether. Its rays reach *them* when their healing is spent. They are conscious of this, and they seek relief in rites and observances, and a quarterly recast of their theological belief. Some of them get so far away as to mistake their CREED for their CHRIST, and to rest their hope that their correctness of BELIEF will answer in lieu of purity of LIFE. But their efforts are of no avail. They are dying AT THE HEART. And while the Saviour pities, He is powerless. They have a darling habit which they have kept back—a part of them which they have not made over— and this it is which eats like a canker into their souls and makes them spiritually impotent. For myself I would rather be the agent by whom the Christians of the United States should be induced to EAT AND DRINK AND DRESS to the glory of God, than to set in motion any plan for the world's redemption of which I can now imagine. It is a settled point with me, that the great indifference to physical laws, or as we term them, the Laws of Life, which the redeemed show, the impunity with which they are violated, the almost universal substitution of holy desires and pious aims in the future, for consecrated life in the present, is a mighty obstacle in His way who is yet to be King of Nations as He is King of Saints."

But if the Saviour be "powerless" WHILE "a part of them" is not "made over," He is not powerless when once the appetite is consecrated to Him. We once knew a minister who, from childhood, had been excessively fond of pastry of nearly all kinds. At length he became convinced that indulgence was detrimental to his health, and promptly refused the enjoyment. But he found that the sight of the luxury created such a craving as to be disagreeable and often led him to break over his self-prescribed limitations

This induced him to pray for the removal of the craving, and it was done, so that the objects of previous desire were no longer a temptation.

Unquestionably, his experience in this regard may be the experience of every one who finds his "easily besetting sin" upon the ta le of Providential Mercies.

It is not our purpose to go into the details of dietetic science, and show the obvious departures from its dicta, in the common practice of the people, but, simply to proclaim, with all the emphasis that the truths already uttered can impart, that the most thorough self control is attainable. Not only so, but the most rigid regimen of the extreme dietarians is *enjoyable* beyond the common indulgences of the table, by reason of the added zest of a healthful appetite, and the pleasurable workings of a mind unclogged by an over-supply of nutriment, and the presence of waste material that should have been excreted.

In adducing the evidence now before the reader, the several criteria named upon pp. 7, 8, by which to estimate the value of testimony, have been kept in view, and it is believed that an array of *facts* is here presented which cannot fail to convince every unprejudiced mind.

The responsibility of acting in accordance with this conviction now devolves upon the reader.

Desiring to be helpful as far as possible to his efforts at self-improvement, we append a sermon, which has been a blessing to many, as an appropriate conclusion to this treatise.

THE WONDROUS NAME.

A

SERMON

Preached at the Messiah Camp Meeting, Milford, Conn., Aug. 15, 1873.

By

REV. S. H. PLATT, A. M.,

Author of "The Gift of Power," "Christ and Adornments," "The Philosophy of Christian Holiness," "Christian Separation from the World," "The Man of Like Passions," "The Christian Law of Giving," "Princely Manhood," Etc.

THIRD EDITION.

Brooklyn, N. Y.
S. HARRISON & CO.
1874.

INTRODUCTION.

On the 1st of September, 1865, the author preached upon the Milford Camp Ground, and by unanimous request of the Ministers present, the Sermon was published as "THE PHILOSOPHY OF CHRISTIAN HOLINESS," and the entire edition of twenty-three hundred copies was sold within three weeks after its issue. When the call was received for the publication of the present Sermon the author felt a degree of constraint to comply growing out of the singular sale and usefulness of that. Nor, can he do better now than to quote the concluding paragraphs from its introductory page:

"But the question at once arose, whether it should be written, as nearly as might be, as it was preached, from the brief notes used—or whether it should be entirely remodeled and appear as a finished production. After much consideration it has been decided to reproduce it as a Sermon, in the belief that whatever faults of arrangement, or otherwise, might thus be repeated, would be conpensated by its freshness and spirit.

"Such as it is, it goes forth with earnest prayer that its usefulness may answer the expectations of the brethren whose kind regards have given it being."

The "Philosophy of Christian Holiness" is now in course of preparation for the press as a 12 mo. vol.

S. H. PLATT.

THE WONDROUS NAME.

"Thou shalt call his name Jesus; for he shall save his people from their sins.—MATT. 1: 21.

AMONG the Jews proper names were significant of qualities, or commemorative of events. Esther—"beautiful," and Naomi—"pleasant," are examples of the first class, while Jacob—"supplanter," and Israel—"prevailing," are of the second; but, in the text both classes seem to be combined, for in the person of Jesus were the QUALITIES of a Saviour, and in his life and death the EVENT of Salvation was accomplished. "Thou shalt call his name Jesus; for he shall save his people from their sins."

We inquire then—

I. WHOM HE WOULD SAVE? And the answer is, "His people." But who are they? Doubtless all those in whom his saving power could be consistently exercised. This includes—

TRUSTING PENITENTS, who, in self-abasement, exclaim with the poor publican, "God, be merciful to me a Sinner!" or cry out with the broken-hearted jailor, "What must I do to be saved?" or, even tremulously answer, with the gleamings of Hope amid Despair, "No man, Lord!" in the language of the uncondemned Adulteress—made penitent and saved by matchless Mercy.

RETURNING WANDERERS, "while yet a great way off," like the half-starved, home-sick, and sin-sick Prodigal, though yet in their rags, and their studied words of Confession yet unspoken, may find ONE falling "upon their necks and kissing them welcome to the old-time home, and the long true hearts of the once spurned, but now sought-for rest.

STRUGGLING BELIEVERS, who have awakened to the painful consciousness of inward perversities, strong leanings of the nature towards sinful thoughts and deeds, and who cry out, in the bewilderment of desperate soul wrestlings with self, "Who shall deliver me from the body of this death?" may surely listen hopefully to this NAME-GOSPEL of the text, "Thou shalt call his name Jesus, for he shall save his people from their sins!"

But let us inquire more particularly—

II. FROM WHAT HE WOULD SAVE THEM? "From their Sins." Sin is a wrong determination of a free will; but, for the sake of impression, we will classify sins mainly by the circumstances of their actual commission. The first species which we notice may be termed SINS OF SURPRISE; as, when well circumstanced Solicitation comes suddenly into unexpected adjustment with Desires already kindled, or with Inclinations on the alert for opportunity. Such was the experience of a friend of former years, who, after desperate struggles, was reformed from a life of inebriety. The fire-alarm hastily called him from his bed at an early hour of a bitter winter morning, to wrestle with the fire-fiend in his might, and nobly did he do his duty until his exhausted frame stood shivering in the blast, his clothes frozen into icy encasements upon him— *then*, just when a cup of strong coffee would have been strength and life, misguided friends passed the punch pail from hand to hand, and it came to his; he tasted and fell; fell as thousands stronger than he have fallen by the ignited spark of Solicitation dropping within the magazine of waiting passion! Ah! how few have been the deliverances that WE have KNOWN, amid the multitude that have been effected for us by a kindly watchful Providence, in shielding us from such Sins of Surprise!

The very best of us have been in ambush often enough to have sealed us over for the pit had not God's loving hand interposed just at the right juncture to snatch us from the peril, or to cover us when the arrows flew. *Salvation is of God's Hand in the circumstances of our lives, as well as of His Grace in the experience of our hearts!*

Again, There are SINS OF VACILLATION, arising chiefly from an unstable mental constitution, like that of Ephraim, "Unstable as water, thou shalt not excel!" Some are born so unfortunately constituted that they seem incapable of any fixed purpose of life, but are ever veering, like weather-vanes, to every change of influence that sweeps across them. It would be strange indeed, if such were not oft-times decoyed into forbidden paths. I was once on my way to visit such a man, who, the evening before had placed himself among the penitents, when I was hailed by a member of my church who inquired where I was going. "To see Mr. ——," said I. "Oh! well, you need not trouble yourself about him, for if he gets converted he will backslide next summer. He has claimed to be converted fifteen times already." "Well," said I, "let us try him the sixteenth time, and perhaps the Lord will take him to heaven before he has time to backslide again." Sure enough, the next summer his old vacillation returned, and was followed the succeeding winter by a renewal of his efforts, and he DIED IN THE COMFORTS OF FAITH before another summer came. That incident taught me a lesson of charity towards the poor victims of mental instability, which has given me hope even in their seventeenth or seventieth effort to seek

Him who has commanded us to forgive unto the seventieth time.

Next, we note SINS OF DEFICIENCY!—when the energies are too slothful, or the will is too timid to meet the emergencies of life. When opportunities that will never return are declined; when duties brimming with Destiny are evaded; and when Crosses planted in the pathway to crowns are not borne for want of a will that dares to attempt, or of energies with vigor to accomplish.

Over against these Sins of Deficiency, at the opposite pole of experience, are SINS OF EXCESSIVE ACTIVITY; as, when a single faculty usurps control over the mind and drives it in the direction of its own function until its normal sphere is transcended, and some degree of perversion ensues. Thus, mirthfulness becomes levity by excess; moral discriminations, assuming judgeship, degenerate into censoriousness; the social propensities fly off, in a fever of indulgence, into the passion of sociality; acquisitiveness withers into miserly greed, and even conscientiousness, super-sensitive, becomes an unsparing hand of scourges to its possessor.

Closely in the wake of Sins of Excess, and partaking largely of their nature, are SINS OF PERVERTED JUDGMENT. As, when the competing claims of worldly and religious interests are deliberately settled in favor of business rather than of religious services, and the tide of secularity is permitted to roll, from Monday morning till Saturday midnight unchecked by a single hour of spiritual exercise, until its mere momentum projects it far into the thoughts of the Sabbath rest. As, when Prudence and Consistency are despoiled of all their charms, that Fashion may be decked in stolen drapery and walk beside the altars of the Lord beguiling his sons and daughters into the paths of vanity and pride. As, when the solemn vows and obligations of baptism and church communion are nullified by the world-inspired opinions of a Laodicean piety, and a Christ-dishonoring judgment gives verdict in favor of the treachery.

Then come SINS OF PROCLIVITY, when the bent of the nature crowds toward some specific indulgence, either because of its constitutional make-up, that is—the relative poise of its several parts; or because of some inheritance of evil by which the particular tendency has been implanted as an inborn habit of the mind. In either case it is the "easily besetting sin" that has become matter of painful experience to multitudes who are in quest of a purer life.

SINS OF ACQUIRED HABITS throng all the avenues of life; and whether the product of excessive development of natural functions, such as irritability, vanity, gluttony, lust, &c., or, the result of voluntary abnormal perversions, as in the appetite for Rum, Tobacco, Opium, &c.— in either case its persistent influence haunts like a spectre, clings like a relentless pain, and holds with a grip of such tremendous power that it unmans manliness, dethrones the sovereignty of will, and threatens to abjure the power of grace itself.

Scarcely less to be deplored are—SINS OF THE PHYSICAL ORGANISM, from some peculiar condition of tissue, blood, or nerve. As when over-stimulated combativeness plants itself in the attitude of hostility ; a conjested liver breeds doubts and despondency ; over-wrought nerves beget irritability, and the processes of animal life inspire lustful desire. Of these, and of all their kin, it is said, "Sin when it is conceived, bringeth forth death." Yet they entail guilt, and are death producing only when their impulsions are indorsed by the will, THEN SIN is conceived. But how easy the transition ! How great the probability of a flame when the spark kindles the combustibles of the physical organism ! What then can be done? Hark ! Away amid the Galilean hills, an angel, radiant with the light of heaven, bends over the couch of the sleeping Joseph and bids him, "Fear not to take unto thee Mary thine espoused, for that which is conceived in her is of the Holy Ghost. And she shall bring forth a son, and thou shalt call his name Jesus ; for he shall save his people from their sins."

If this be true—

III. *Upon what terms will he save them ?*

First there must be ABSOLUTE SUBMISSION. "Whosoever will be my disciple, let him deny himself and take up his cross and follow me." Battle array broken; colors struck; arms grounded;—unconditional surrender FIRST!! Then—

Second, UNRESERVED CONSECRATION. "Render unto Cæsar the things that be Cæsar's, and unto GOD the THINGS THAT BE GOD'S.—Luke 20:25. Do you ask what are his? "Ye are not your own, for ye are bought with a price; therefore glorify God in your body, and in your spirit, WHICH ARE GOD'S.—1 Cor. 6: 19-20. Body and spirit have been bought with a price! Body and spirit belong to God! He claims his own; and consecration without reservation honors the claim; but it must be a giving away of self so completely that not even the right to take back the gift is retained, then does it become the "LIVING SACRIFICE holy and acceptable unto God, which is your reasonable service."

Then comes, Third, CORRESPONDING APPROPRIATION. Without faith it is impossible to please Him; for he that cometh to God must believe that He is, and that He is the REWARDER of them that diligently seek Him."—Heb. 11 : 6. They who seek God in thorough submission and entire consecration do unquestionably "DILIGENTLY seek Him" What, then, is their REWARD? As unquestionably as before—the object of their search—God. But He is apprehended only by faith; hence, an appropriation by faith corresponding with the gift rendered to Him, is the next legitimate step! For, if consecration has any value, it conditionates acceptance. Hence CORRESPONDING APPROPRIATION means reliance upon Him to take ALL that consecration gives, and just WHEN it gives, and just as LONG as it gives!! This done, and there must be—

Fourth, CONTINUOUS CLINGING! Reliance perpetuated by repeated acts of will, as life is prolonged by successive acts of breathing. "Ye have need of PATIENCE, that after ye have done the will of God, ye might receive the promise.—Heb. 10: 36. Clinging to him in the consciousness of having done his will by submission, and consecration, and appropriation, you are to keep on clinging until your patience is rewarded by the promised baptism of the Holy Ghost giving assurance and joy.

But, if we do all that He requires—

IV. *To what extent will He save?*

First—To the Boundaries of His own Munificence!

Creation, preservation, redemption, and salvation reveal its breadth and height.

He creates like a God!

He speaks, and worlds roll forth from his hand and range into systems, and systems marshal into the ranks of the universe,—the first as numberless as the last is limitless, and all flashing in the dewy splendors of creation's morn, reveal the munificence of His creating power.

He upholds like a God!

Through all the realms of nature, causes fail not to run into effects, laws cease not their sovereign sway, life's countless forms emerge in beauty from the shades of death, and all the processes of vitality, in wondrous combination roll their rounds of marvelous adjustment, till earth and air and sky are flooded with the harmonies of being. Oh, the munificence of Nature's God!

Yon apple-tree asked for a thousand apples, and Nature decked it with a million blossoms, each germinal of fruit. This forest asked for leaves, and this beautiful dome of living green was deftly spread by unseen hands upon the boughs till every twig danced for very joy. The fields ask for herbage, and they are carpeted with grass till velvet lawns and verdant meadows evoke the sports of childhood, and reward the sons of toil. Life asks for air, and an Ærial Ocean eleven times higher than the highest mountain on which life dares to dwell is God's answering supply. The earth asks for sunbeams, and they come blazing through the depths of space, shimmering amid our leafy canopy, gleaming across our pathway, shooting into dells, and glancing from mountain peaks till the very heavens are all aglow with the fiery radiance.

Nor is this all. For yonder sun is not so niggardly as to bless our earth alone. No! No! On EVERY SIDE—far out into the regions of infinite space, wherever the swift wings of Light can cleave the unbroken darkness of immensity, there the sun pours his ceaseless tides of golden glory till the Universe is aflame with his munificence of splendor. Faint emblem of the munificence of its God!

HE REDEEMS LIKE A GOD!

He might have been content with furnishing redemption for Adam and Eve alone, or for a certain favored few of their descendants. But no! He would cover the earth with tribes and nations, till a countless generation should cry out of the depths of their sinful wretchedness for help! He would roll generation after generation through their brief space of life, until the steady tramp of the Ages halts at the bivouac of judgment, and the myriads of earth's sons respond to the roll call of Eternity—and then challenge the Spirit of Evil to point to a SINGLE ONE not redeemed with blood! Oh, the lavish wealth of Redeeming Love!!

> "Lord, I believe were sinners more
> Than sands upon the Ocean shore,
> Thou hast for EACH a ransom paid.—
> For all a full atonement made!"

AND HE SAVES LIKE A GOD!

Redemption is provisional; salvation

is efficient. Consisting in a marvelous moral reconstruction, with a contemporaneous external revolution—too mighty for any inferior power, too precious for any lesser love, too glorious for any sullied purity.

Salvation in its nature is divine! And of its extent we read—"He is able to save unto the uttermost!" Let us read that again. To be SAVED is a glorious thing —almost surpassing human belief; but here is a measure given. Not only will he save, but "He will save unto———" what? My wish? My sense of need? No, not that;—beyond that, for that may fall far short of my real necessity—UNTO THE UTTERMOST!

Unto the UTTER is the left hand boundary of WANT! Unto the MOST is the right hand boundary of NEED! But UTTER and MOST—both superlatives—are here conjoined into ONE COMPOUND SUPER-SUPERLATIVE to express all possibilities of need lying between the center and the circumference of probationary existence! Oh, how language groans to express the munificence of God's salvation!

But Paul does not stop here. He gives another turn to the rack, and tortures out another conglomeration of qualifying words which crown him as the very king of sublime and glorious expression. Listen! "God is able." Take care, good Paul; he who launches out upon God's ABILITY, has a far-off shore to reach before he can bound it, and tell its sum! But hear with what unfaltering tones he rings out —"God is able to make GRACE ABOUND." Yes, yes, we know that, blessed be His Name! (But stop! A word has fallen out.) "God is able to make ALL GRACE abound toward you." Hallelujah! That is glorious! "ALL GRACE?" that must be grace in sufficient measure, and for every extremity. Yes, and it "ABOUNDS!" There is not only enough, but an overflow,—a surplusage—munificence of supply! "Hold!" I seem to hear Paul saying, "Don't go off in ecstacies yet; wait until I finish. Hear now!"—"God is able"—(That is so good that he has to repeat it every time)—"to make all grace abound toward you ; that ye always"—having SUFFICIENCY ? No ! "having ALL SUFFICIENCY in ALL THINGS MAY ABOUND TO EVERY GOOD WORK." Enough, my Lord, enough! Thou dost save like a God!

Second. HE SAVES TO THE LIMITS OF HUMAN NEED. That need is indicated by the sinfulness of the needy one. Here are the SURPRISED ONES who once wore the crown of moral worth, and rejoiced in an integrity unsullied as the sun, but in an unexpected hour they fell, and great was the fall! But a GREATER SAVIOUR we proclaim to-day ; one who "knoweth how to deliver out of temptation," and clothe in an armor in which ye "shall be able to stand against the wiles of the devil," while, for all your past, He will "forgive its iniquity, transgression, and sin."

Here are UNSTABLE ONES—tossed to-day upon the tide of religious influence, to-morrow drifting off upon the eddying flood of worldliness—anon stranded waifs awaiting another freshet season to bear them onward toward the haven. Hear ye! "In returning and REST shall ye be saved; in quietness and in confidence shall be your strength."—Isa. 30:15.

Here are TIMID and LAGGARD ONES—the one too fearful, and the other too indolent to reap the golden harvests of ripened opportunity, and garner the blessed sheaves of God's confiding Providence. Listen, ye fearful! "He it is that doth go before thee, He will be with thee; fear not, neither be dismayed.—Deut. 31:8.

Hear, and tremble, O ye laggard ones! "Strive to enter in at the straight gate, for many shall seek to enter, and shall not be able." "Except your righteousness exceed the righteousness of the Scribes and Pharisees, ye shall in no case enter into the kingdom of heaven."

Here are STRAYING ONES—who plunge into excesses of levity, censoriousness, sociality, &c., till their lives are spotted all over with inconsistencies, their eyes are blurred to all glorious prospects, and their hearts barred from all triumphant joy, while a weeping Saviour plaintively pleads—"If thou wouldest seek unto God betimes, and make thy supplication unto the Almighty; if thou wert pure and upright, surely now he would awake for thee, and make the habitation of thy righteousness prosperous."—Job, 8 : 5. And the inspiring spirit cheerily proclaims, "I will teach you the good and the right way; only fear the Lord, and love him in truth with all thine heart; for consider how great things he hath done for you."—1 Sam. 12 : 23.

Here are WORDLY BIASSED ONES—so steeped in the narcotizing power of greed, that, like tobacco slaves, they cling to their disgusting quid rather than suck the luscious peach of week-day religious services of prayer and song, and their perverted judgments endorse their preference, and justify their iniquity! They are "turned aside like a deceitful bow," and of them God says, "Because ye are turned away from the Lord, therefore the Lord will not be with you."—Numb. 14 : 43.

Here are those with INBORN PERVERSITIES—proclivities to evil so reprobate that they seem begotten of the devil, and hunger, like death, for pollution; proclivities that so take hold on hell, that attraction and affinity and momentum all impel with infernal power toward the pit. Hear! ye fiend-crowded, passion-goaded victims, hear!! The strong hand of omnipotent arrest is by your side, the spirit of Divine assurance pulses in the air, while, sweetly as the voice of benediction soundeth in your ears, "My grace is sufficient for thee ; for my strength is made perfect in weakness."—2 Cor. 12 : 9.

Here are HABIT-ENSLAVED ONES—some in the mad whirl of an excitement as unreasoning as it is unfearing ; some hugging their manacles of steel, and delusively deeming them golden symbols of royalty; some yielding protestingly, like overpersuaded virtue in the arms of vice ; some chafing like caged lions against their bars; and others breaking desperately out of their environments like spring freshets over confining banks, only to subside to a hopeless imprisonment again; ALL, fettered and enslaved, yet fit subjects of an emancipation, richer and more glorious than ever emblazoned the page of secular history, and found only in those finite clingings to the Infinite which exclaim, "I can do all things through Christ strengthening me!"— Phil. 4 : 13

Here are victims of DISEASED OR PERVERTED ORGANIZATIONS,—hanging a pall of despondency over the earth, and veiling out the glories of the sky by the mists of doubt; or, irritable as the charged battery answering with a spark of fire to every adverse touch, or lusting, like the open grave to find their fill of pollution,— goaded, lashed, frenzied, hell-struck by desire,—the barriers of judgment worn down by mere attrition, conscience worried out by ceaseless strife, the opposition of the better nature trampled beneath the heels of the massed charge of wild, rampant passion! Good heavens, what a life! But hark! The glorious old Apostle to the Gentiles—(those people steeped in corruption and rotten to the core,) is ready for us as well as for them, as he hurls across the seething gulf of human perversities the God-given assurance. (1 Cor. 10 : 13.) "God is FAITHFUL who will not suffer you to be tempted above that ye are able ; but will, with the temptation, also MAKE A WAY TO ESCAPE, that ye may be able to bear it."

"Make way for liberty!" was the commanding challenge of Switzerland's noble son, as he gathered in his arms and cushioned in his heart a score of the thirsty spear-points of his country's embattled foes.

Liberty rushed through the broken ranks of leveled weapons, and Switzerland was free ! !

"Make a way to escape !" was the sentiment of the dying Son of God as he bared his heart to all the barbed darts of darkness ; and charging ranks of deliverance have ever since swept through that breach to the rescue of the trusting, tempted ones !

Now, I proclaim to all whom sin has blighted, and guilt has cursed,—a name, a Jewish name! with meaning in every letter, and a world of significance in its whole— *Jesus*, JESUS, JESUS!

Hear his promise by Isaiah (43: 1 2. "Fear not, for I have redeemed thee; I have called thee by thy NAME"—(Blessed particularity of application!) "Thou art mine," (Glorious assurance!) "When thou passest through the waters I will be with thee,"(Precious company!) "And through the rivers, they shall not overflow thee;" (Restful promise!) "When thou walkest through the fire, thou shalt not be burned," (Divine protection!) "Neither shall the flame kindle upon thee!" Hallelujah! Like the three Hebrew children there shall not be even the smell of fire upon our garmets! Glory be to God! Ah! Paul has found his match at last? That regal old Prophet of Israel plucked fire from Heaven when he caught the inspiration of that peerless PROMISE OF THE AGES. But hold! We do the Apostle an injustice. Let him try; and here he comes swinging GOD'S ABILITY once more as his battle-ax of promise for the world, and his clear tones ring out most jubilantly—"He is ABLE." (What an emphasis he puts upon that word able!) "to do all that we ask." There, he is BROADER than Isaiah, already; "or THINK!" Now he soars, and is almost out of sight, but he drops a qualifying word. "He is able to do ABOVE all that we ask or think." But tell us, dear Paul, that we may see how like a God he saves, tell us, how much above? And now he bends those climacteric pinions toward us just enough to launch forth one of those infinite words of his—"ABUNDANTLY ABOVE!" O, my soul! catch a glimmering, if thou canst, of the majestic, boundless amplitude of HIS ABILITY! Quickly! for Paul's lips move once more, and now the very heavens rend with the expansion of the thought, and through the rift we seem to see the infinite pulsations of Jehovah's might as Paul claps the crown upon the climax—"*He is able to do above all that we can ask or think*, EXCEEDING ABUNDANTLY."

Who can wonder, now, that he throws in, as a sort of practical deduction,—that audacious prayer! "And the very God of peace sanctify you wholly ; and I pray God your whole spirit and soul and body be preserved BLAMELESS unto the coming of our Lord Jesus Christ !"—1 Thess. 5 : 23-24.

If, then, He will thus save—

V. *When will He save?*

First, Just when you comply with the terms.

"This is the confidence that we have in him, that if we ask anything according to his will," (and certainly asking for salvation in compliance with his terms is "according to his will,") "he heareth us! and if we know that he hears us, whatsoever we ask, we know that we HAVE the petitions that we desire of him."—1 John 5 : 14-15.

If this be not enough, behold Paul's new setting of that gem of Old Testament assurance—"I have heard thee in the time accepted ; in the day of salvation I have succored thee : behold, NOW is the time accepted, TO-DAY is the day of salvation."

The sunlight struggling at the closed shutters ; the home-sick school-boy waiting the word—"Come home!" the convalescent soldier with a furlough in his hand ; the imprisoned convict tear-blinded and trembling at news of executive pardon—these need no prompting ! Throw wide the barriers, and the sunlight leaps joyfully to fill every crevice with its smile ; "My boy come home !"—written upon the top of the page, and not even Father's letter will be read through before the boy is ready for the start.

So, Jesus Christ waits no second invitation ! Hurl away the barriers ; call out —"Come in !"—and, quicker than the lightning's flash, the God head's struggling Love shall fill, illuminate, and save !

Are you SUBMISSIVE now ? Haul down the colors of pride, and " Come out from among them and be ye separate."

Do you CONSECRATE now ? It is nothing less than purposed devotion of heart and service to God, from this instant—forevermore. It is the use of every faculty in its rightful functions, for His glory. You have a faith faculty. In the gift of all to Him, have you included this ? If so, it must be exercised believingly

THIS MOMENT, for that is its legitimate and most sacred function.

You have given ALL to Him; now, it is the crowning act of consecration—rather, it is the first legitimate act springing from a consecrated state, to believe that He accepts all that you give. It is faith-faculty in consecrated use!

Do you then—APPROPRIATE just now? God asked the gift. You made it, and now lie unresisting in His hands.

Will He, CAN HE stand holding your guilty, sin-stained soul in the hollow of His palm, looking at it on every side, but DOING NOTHING FOR IT? No! No! A thousand times *No!* All the instincts of His purity, all the promptings of His love, all the impulses of His truthfulness impel Him INSTANTLY to plunge beneath the cleansing Blood every polluted soul thus helpless and expectant in his hands. Away, then, with doubt! A soul consciously given to God through all its known powers and susceptibilities IS SAVED THEN AND THERE to the full extent of the consecration itself.

There may be, just then, no sensible

change, no manifested evidence, but as surely as its saved state is assumed by faith, without other evidence than the promise of God and its own conscious fulfillment of the conditions of acceptance, so surely will the event justify its confidence.

Secondly, He saves JUST AS LONG as you comply with the terms. Do you now submit and consecrate yourselves? Then let Paul speak for you yet again—"I know whom I have believed, and am persuaded that He is able." (How he rings the changes on God's ability!) "To KEEP *that* which I have COMMITTED unto Him against that day."

Are you APPROPRIATING? Let Isaiah speak once more—"Israel shall be saved in the Lord with an EVERLASTING Salvation, ye shall not be ASHAMED or CONFOUNDED WORLD WITHOUT END!"—Chap. 45:12.

Are you CLINGING? The kingly Prophet has words of cheer. "Thou wilt keep him in perfect peace whose mind is STAYED ON THEE, because he TRUSTETH in thee. Trust ye in the Lord FOREVER, for in the

Lord Jehovah is everlasting strength."—Isa. 26 : 3-4.

"But I am only clinging!" cries a timid one—"That promise is for those who are STAYED on Him!" Granted; but good old Isaiah has not delved in the mines of divine thought so long without finding a promise cut and carved expressly for the clinging. Listen! "Fear thou not, for I am with thee, be not dismayed for I am thy God; I will *strengthen* thee; yea, I will HELP thee, yea, I will UPHOLD thee with the right hand of my righteousness."—Isa. 41 : 10.

What better can the shipwrecked sailor ask, while clinging to the life-boat, than to be STRENGTHENED and UPHELD and HELPED? And the effect of God's upholdings is precisely what your hearts are groaning after. Hear Isaiah once more—"The work of righteousness shall be peace, and the effect of righteousness—quietness and assurance forever!"—Isa. 32 : 17.

Here, clinging one, is a resting place, secure and satisfying, for Paul comes around again declaring—"He hath said, I will never leave thee, nor forsake thee!"

—Heb. 13 : 5. And, to make assurance doubly sure, The Psalmist chimes in—"The Lord shall preserve thee from all evil; he shall preserve thy soul. The Lord shall preserve thy GOING OUT, and thy COMING IN, from THIS TIME FORTH, and even FOREVERMORE !!!"— Psa. 121 : 7-8.

Now, let us harness submission, consecration, appropriation, and clinging before the chariot of this blood bought opportunity, and puting the reins in the hands of faith, drive to the skies over the "highway of holiness cast up" (above the mire of earth, and the pollutions of sin) "for the ransomed of the Lord." "*His name shall be called Jesus, for he shall save his people from their sins !*"

Come ye bruised and mangled ones,—scathed and scorched by the fires of passion, smitten and withered by guilt, and longing after rest. Come to Jesus!

And ye, aspring ones,—heart sick with a life so inferior to your ideal,—shrinking from the clammy touch of a pollution that is "flesh of your flesh," and with a great inward void aching with unutterable longings to be filled with God,—come to Jesus! Come one, come ALL, and while your Past rolls under the blood, and your Present clings to the uplifted Christ, spread your Future out broadly upon the Divine promises, and standing beside the Cross, lift up your voices in the supreme confidence of Isaiah's faith when he exclaimed—(chap. 50 : 7) "The Lord God will help me, therefore shall I not be confounded ; therefore have I set my face like a flint, and I KNOW THAT I SHALL NOT BE ASHAMED!"

ADVERTISEMENTS.

Elijah, the Tishbite.

BY REV. S. H. PLATT, A. M

AUTHOR OF

"The Gift of Power," etc.

The grandest life in Ancient History was that of the Tishbite Prophet. This is a pen-portrait of that MAN OF FIRE, drawn in colors vivid as the lightnings of his mountain home, and revealing the SOURCES of his POWER, and the GLORY of his CHARACTER.

It is a MIGHTY INSPIRATION toward the noblest type of manhood, and the loftiest ideal of Christian excellence!

A critic, charmed with its style, has pronounced it "A PROSE POEM."

Fifty-four pages, printed on superfine, double calendered, best quality of tinted book paper.

Sent to any address, post-paid, for 20 cents, by

S. HARRISON & CO.,

BROOKLYN, N. Y.

ADVERTISEMENTS.

Princely Manhood.

A Private Treatise on the Procreative Instinct, as Related to Moral and Christian Life.

FOR ADULTS ONLY—OF BOTH SEXES.

BY

REV. S. H. PLATT, A. M.

Author of "The Gift of Power;" "Christ and Adornments;" "Christain Separation from the World;" "The Philosophy of Christian Holiness;" "The Man of Like Passions;" "To Every Man his Work;" "The Christian Law of Giving;" "The Wondrous Name;" "The Power of Grace," etc.

This is a work of rare interest and value to every *adult*. There are but *few* who do not *need* it, and *all* may be greatly *profited* by it. It fills a sphere hitherto unoccupied. *Happiness and salvation for two worlds are in its pages!*

Husbands and wives should procure it for each other; the bethrothed should receive it from parents; brothers and sisters should present it to each other; friends should hand it to friends; pastors should put it into the hands of converts; teachers should advise its perusal by adult pupils.—*Such is the verdict of thoughtful and unprejudiced minds.*

Sent post-paid to any address, for 50 cents; muslin 60 cents, by

S. HARRISON & CO., Brooklyn, N. Y.

Publishers of Rev. S. H. Platt's Works.

INDEX TO PRINCELY MANHOOD.

	PAGE.
Appetite—Sexual, most craving	7
" instruct children concerning	97
" knowledge of will come	97
Adultery	39
Abstinence, amative, pleasure of	81
Aim, singleness of in christian life	65
Affections, ministered to in copulation	9
Amativeness has legitimate sphere	45, 47
" size of the organ in childhood and maturity	49, 52
" early ripening of	50
Appetites, may be mastered by grace	101
Brain disease from self-abuse	21
Bible-doctrine concerning sex	38
"Burn,"	41
Bondage of Christian life to sexuality	66
Ballet panders to pollution	101
Continence, contented	110
Consecration of generative functions	91, 107
Conservation of mental and physical energies,	93
Cleanliness important	107
Consecration of Faculties	66
Christian life, in its elements	65
" " " " longings and strivings	66
" " " " Possibilities of,	67

INDEX TO PRINCELY MANHOOD.

	PAGE
Conception, avoiding	12
Continence	40
"Cannot contain,"	42
Connubial rights, reciprocal	43
Conjugal obligation	43
Continence, gift of	40
Desire should be made *impersonal*	108
Desires, excitement of to be avoided	102
Directions, practical to the married	101
" " " " unmarried	105
Devotedness to God increased	94
Delirium-tremens of lust	54
Digestive ailments from self-abuse	21
Divorce	38
Desires, sexual, not enemies	87
Experience, Lessons of	48
Excesses, Matrimonial	31
" " diseases from	33
" " cause loss of love	34
" " beget puny children	35
Eunuchs, natural	39
" mutilated	39
" voluntarily continent	40
Enticing reveries	105
Fornication, to avoid	11
Faith in Christ as a present Saviour	91
Genital disease from self-abuse	20
Grace, course of in sexuality	90
Healed, by faith	78
Harmony of sexual instinct with Purity	85
" how attained	86
" " preserved	91
" result of	92

INDEX TO PRINCELY MANHOOD.

PAGE

Information, sexual, where found	4
Instinct, sexual, explained	6
" " design of	9
" " perversions of	15
" " Bible doctrine of	38
Indulgence, God to be glorified in	105
" exposure in	29
" thoughts of not allowed	81
" must minister to affection	104
Inefficiency, spiritual, resulting from the warfare against desire	55
Inheritance, conditions of safe	95
Licentiousness, power of	24
" hopelessness of	25
" fearful risks of	26
Lust, look of forbidden	44
" struggles of	55
" warfare with, a cause of disease	55
Liberties, thoughts of	102
Manhood, princely, importance of	3
Modesty, true	5
" spurious	5
Marriage, not good	39, 42
" not demeaned by " necessity,"	46
" bed, satisfaction of, God's provision	46
Non-celibatists, necessary	42
" Necessity" for indulgence	42, 46
" Necessity" a call of God's Providence	46
Nervous fluid, waste of in amativeness	51
Nymphomania	52
Nymphomania, effects of	53
Nature, course of in sexuality	89
Organs, sexual	6

INDEX TO PRINCELY MANHOOD.

	PAGE.
Ownership, reciprocal bodily	102
Opportunity and importunity	106
Passion-wants	12
Pregnancy prevented	13
Prostitution	23
" prevalence of	24
Pure, all things	45
Purity, heart, ethereal	47
Pernicious Literature	99
" " striking example of	100
" " terrible power of	100
Rest of soul in right sexual relations	84
" " " inspiring experience of	80
" " " glorious	93
" " " in contented continence	110
Reveries, lustful, may be prevented	90
Rights, personal	102
" of health	103
" of self-respect	103
Species, perpetuation of	9
Self-abuse	15
" prevalence of	16
" " " in both sexes	19
" consequence of	20
Spinal irritation from self-abuse	21
Syphilis	26
" three forms of	27
" infectiousness of	28
" prevalence of	28
" effects of	28
" tortures of	30
Semen, loss of in copulation	31
Satyriasis, fearful effects of	25

INDEX TO PRINCELY MANHOOD.

PAGE.

Sanctified USE of faculties... 67
" DIS-USE of faculties... 67
" " " " thrilling experience of... 68–80
Solicitation to indulgence, power over... 80
Sexual motions cannot be avoided... 88
" tendencies must not be prematurely developed 96
Temptation to be avoided... 91–105
" children to be shielded from... ... 98
" " " taught the significance of 99
Thankfulness for amative sensations. 108
Ulcers, syphilitic... 29
Usefulness enlarged... 94
Virginity, voluntary... 41
Warfare against amative desire... 48
" " " " detailed experience of... 57–64

www.ingramcontent.com/pod-product-compliance
Lightning Source LLC
Chambersburg PA
CBHW020239170426
43202CB00008B/150